The GRAY THREAT

*Assessing the Next-Generation
European Fighters*

Mark Lorell

Daniel P. Raymer

Michael Kennedy

Hugh Levaux

Project AIR FORCE

Prepared for the
United States Air Force

RAND

This report examines the three major new fighter aircraft now under development in Europe—the EF-2000, Rafale, and Gripen—from the perspective of the possible "gray threat" they could pose to U.S. tactical fighter forces deployed in foreign contingencies if those aircraft were acquired by potentially hostile countries outside of Europe. It discusses the probable operational capabilities of the aircraft compared with U.S. fighters, the likelihood that the aircraft will be fully developed and procured, and the prospects for sales outside of Europe.

This study was produced in the Strategy, Doctrine, and Force Structure Program of RAND's Project AIR FORCE as part of a larger strategic appraisal of global developments in air power. It should be of interest to Air Force leaders and planners, others interested in national security issues, students of arms control and conventional arms proliferation, and those interested in the future of aerospace power.

PROJECT AIR FORCE

Project AIR FORCE, a division of RAND, is the Air Force federally funded research and development center (FFRDC) for studies and analyses. It provides the Air Force with independent analyses of policy alternatives affecting the development, employment, combat readiness, and support of current and future aerospace forces. Research is being performed in three programs: Strategy, Doctrine, and Force Structure; Force Modernization and Employment; and Resource Management and System Acquisition.

Project AIR FORCE is operated under Contract F49620-91-C-0003 between the Air Force and RAND.

CONTENTS

FIGURES

TABLES

INTRODUCTION

With the collapse of the Soviet Union, serious questions have been raised about the continuing need for highly capable and extremely expensive weapon systems conceived at the height of the Cold War. Shrinking defense budgets are forcing U.S. defense planners to make difficult and painful decisions about which weapon system R&D programs to retain and which to cancel.

One such weapon system under increasing scrutiny is the Lockheed/Boeing F-22, the future premier air-superiority fighter planned for the U.S. Air Force. Is the continued development and full procurement of the F-22 still necessary? Does the increasingly unlikely prospect of the emergence of a next-generation Russian fighter over the next decade undermine the basic rationale for the F-22? This report responds to these questions with a resounding "no," after carefully examining the "gray threat" posed to the U.S. tactical fighter force by three advanced fighter aircraft and their munitions now under development in Europe: the multinational Eurofighter EF-2000, the French Rafale, and the Swedish Gripen.

In their defense of the F-22 program, Air Force and Defense Department officials have often pointed to the likely future proliferation of "gray threats," the next-generation European fighter aircraft that are highly capable and are likely to be widely exported. Without the F-22, it is argued, U.S. forces might have to confront an opponent who, through the purchase of one of these new European aircraft, could field a weapon system equal or superior to those deployed by American armed forces.

This study contributes to the debate over the F-22 by examining the "gray threat" more analytically and in greater detail than has been typical in the press. It is based on information gathered by a RAND research team that visited European contractors and government agencies in the spring of 1994. Three basic questions about the new European fighters are evaluated:

- How good are they and how much better can they get?
- Will R&D be completed and full-scale production launched?
- Will they be widely exported outside of Europe?

HOW GOOD ARE THE NEW EUROPEAN FIGHTERS?

After a technical description and overview of the three fighters, we review available information regarding the fighters' likely capabilities and combat effectiveness compared with existing U.S. fighters. The evidence indicates that the new European fighters will employ a considerable amount of cutting-edge aerospace technology and are likely to be equipped with an impressive array of subsystems and advanced components. Our estimates of the basic performance data relevant to aerial combat for EF-2000 and Rafale appear to indicate a clear superiority in capability compared with the F-16C Block 40, and essential equivalence with the F-15 in important areas. In terms of air-to-ground capability, the new European fighters appear quite capable. Although none of the European fighters is primarily oriented toward ground-attack operations like the F-15E, the EF-2000 and Rafale are nonetheless particularly impressive in terms of quantity and variety of stores carried. Based on publicly available data, these two fighters appear to be considerably superior to the F-16 in these areas. Maximum external loads for the Rafale surpass 70 percent of the capability of the much larger F-15E strike/fighter.

In our examination of the subsystems and munitions planned for the new fighters, we note that the Europeans are closing the performance gap in many areas. Particularly noteworthy are the RBE2 phased-array fire-control radar planned for the Rafale, the DASS electronic warfare (EW) suite under development for EF-2000, the

French MICA medium-range air-to-air missile, and a variety of other advanced missiles and munitions.

A review of extensive computer combat assessments and simulations conducted by the Europeans seems to indicate that the European fighters are equal or superior to most existing U.S. tactical fighters. At the same time, the review also shows the F-22 to be dramatically more capable than both existing U.S. fighters *and* the new European aircraft. While recommending extreme caution in use of the simulation results, we conclude that they cannot be casually dismissed.

Finally, we discuss European plans for future upgrades and advanced technology developments. The Europeans have extensive plans for significantly improving their aircraft. Of particular note are the widespread efforts under way in Europe to develop new low-observable stealth technologies and apply them to the new fighters.

WILL R&D BE COMPLETED AND PRODUCTION LAUNCHED?

We briefly assess the political and budgetary outlook in each country as it may affect the full development and procurement of the aircraft. Now entering into full-scale production, the Gripen is shown to be in a strong position. A review of current French defense procurement and budget policies suggests that Rafale will almost certainly be fully developed and procured in planned numbers. EF-2000 has been a troubled program, but our examination of the political, military, and budgetary environments in all four member countries indicates that the program will go ahead into production, probably with German participation, but possibly without it.

WILL THEY BE EXPORTED?

To answer this question, we discuss each county's export policies, the likely pricing of the fighters compared to U.S. fighters against which they may compete for foreign sales, and briefly survey the probable non-European market prospects. We conclude that the Europeans will successfully market these fighters outside of Europe because (1) the participating governments and contractors are totally committed to promoting foreign sales, (2) the fighters will be priced competitively with U.S. aircraft, (3) the Europeans will place fewer restrictions on technology transfer than the United States does, and will provide other economic incentives, and (4) a worldwide demand for new fighters exists.

CONCLUSIONS

In conclusion, we believe the "gray threat" is real. The new European fighters provide a powerful argument for full and timely procurement of the F-22 for these reasons:

- With these new fighters, the Europeans appear to be taking a significant step toward closing the traditional performance gap with American fighters. Armed with the appropriate munitions, these fighters and planned upgraded versions are likely to be highly competitive with existing U.S. fighters and future variants, with the notable exception of the F-22.

- It is probable that all three European fighters will be fully developed and produced in significant numbers.

- Despite high price tags and a constrained global market, the three European fighters have a reasonable prospect of winning significant foreign orders.

ACKNOWLEDGMENTS

The authors are grateful to the many European government and aerospace industry officials who provided the authors with considerable information and data without which this report could not have been written. Several stand out for the extensive help and support they provided in the course of this research effort: Hannes Ross, Manager, Advanced Design, Military Aircraft Division, Messerschmitt-Bölkow-Blohm/Deutsche Aerospace, Germany; Carl G. Lundgren, Commercial Directorate, Defense Materiel Administration (FMV), Sweden; John Mabberley, Managing Director (Operations), Defence Research Agency, Farnborough, United Kingdom; and Jean-Louis Gergorin, Member of the Board of Directors, Deputy to the Chairman for Strategic Coordination, Matra-Hachette, France. We would also like to especially thank M. S. Sharland, Project Director, Business Development, British Aerospace Defence; Yves Thiriet, Senior Vice President, Research, Design and Engineering, Dassault Aviation, France; and Tommy Ivarsson, Vice President, Director Strategic Planning, Saab Military Aircraft, Sweden. We are deeply grateful to them, and to all the other individuals in Europe and the United States who shared so generously of their time and knowledge.

Several RAND colleagues made important contributions to this effort. The authors would particularly like to thank Dr. Zalmay Khalilzad, Director of the Strategy, Doctrine, and Force Structure Program, Project AIR FORCE, for his support and encouragement. William Stanley contributed extensive data and analytical insights on the costs of U.S. fighter aircraft. Major Art Huber, RAND Air Force Fellow, provided critical technical expertise and knowledge regarding current developments in U.S. and European tactical missile R&D and operational employment.

This report was formally reviewed by Richard Betts, Director, Institute of War and Peace Studies, Columbia University, and Eliot A. Cohen, Johns Hopkins University Foreign Policy Institute, School of Advanced International Studies. Their suggestions, criticisms, and insights proved to be invaluable.

The authors remain solely responsible for the views expressed in this report, and for any errors that may be found therein.

Chapter One

INTRODUCTION

With the collapse of the Soviet Union and the resulting decline in the U.S. defense budget, Americans are once again engaging in a defense policy debate over the optimal size and mix of military forces necessary to protect vital U.S. security interests around the globe. However, unlike similar debates during the Cold War, the likely future threats are now ill-defined and uncertain. No consensus has yet emerged among politicians and policy analysts for a revamped U.S. political/military strategy necessary for the "new world order" and an appropriate military force structure to back it up.

In this environment of strategic uncertainty and downward pressures on defense spending, costly weapon system procurement programs conceived at the height of the Cold War have come under increasing attack from critics in Congress and elsewhere. One of the primary targets for the post–Cold War budget cutters is the future advanced tactical fighter, the Lockheed/Boeing F-22. This stealthy new fighter is under development for the U.S. Air Force as a replacement for the McDonnell-Douglas F-15C, the Air Force's current premier air superiority fighter. As the only all-new fighter aircraft now planned for acquisition over the next several decades, the F-22 remains the Air Force's highest-priority weapon system procurement program for the 1990s.

Recent budget cuts have already reduced the planned procurement numbers of the F-22 from 750 to 442, a cut of over 40 percent, and delayed anticipated initial operational capability to 2004. Nonetheless, with a currently projected total program cost of $71 billion,[1] the F-22 is still one of the most expensive weapon system procurement programs in the Pentagon's budget, and thus remains vulnerable to attack by those seeking to further reduce defense expenditures. Indeed, as recently as August 1994, senior Defense Department officials warned the Air Force leadership to prepare to stretch out the F-22 program by an additional four years because of budgetary shortfalls.[2]

Opponents of the F-22 program argue that with the disappearance of the Soviet threat and the decline in the Russian military aerospace industry, the U.S. Air Force no longer needs such a high-capability and sophisticated stealth fighter as the F-22, even if it could afford it. This argument seemed to receive a major boost in February 1994, when the GAO (Government Accounting Office) released a long-anticipated report that compared the capability of current U.S. Air Force fighters and the F-22 with the new Russian MFI (Multirole Fighter Interceptor), an extensively upgraded Su-27 Flanker. The report concluded that the F-22 is not needed in the next decade. According to the GAO, the current F-15 will remain roughly comparable to the MFI in most important performance areas, and thus will be adequate to cope with the future threat posed by the new Russian fighter.[3]

Air Force, Defense Department, and industry officials promptly responded to the GAO report with criticisms of its assumptions and methodology. A central component of their counterarguments focused on the GAO's alleged failure to take into account the widespread proliferation of "gray threats": next-generation fighter aircraft and munitions, now under development by European contractors, that are highly capable and likely to be widely exported.[4] Although the developers of these weapon systems are close U.S. allies or friendly neutrals, economic circumstances may force them to export their products to almost any foreign country that can pay for

---

[1]Then-year dollars spent for procurement of total buy when production ends in 2013. See Theresa Hitchens and Robert Holzer, "USAF Explores Panoply of F-22 Derivatives," *Defense News*, August 1–7, 1994.

[2]*Los Angeles Times*, August 22, 1994.

[3]"Air Force Faults GAO on F-22 Study," *Aerospace Daily*, March 28, 1994.

[4]Air Force officials have also argued that Russia is developing a new highly capable air superiority fighter that is likely to be widely sold abroad.

them. According to the U.S. Air Force, fighters such as the multi-national EF-2000 or Eurofighter,[5] the French Rafale, and the Swedish Gripen "will have significant speed, stealth and maneuverability improvements over current types, and . . . are actively being marketed worldwide."[6] Supporters of the F-22 claim that the new European fighters will be significantly more capable in agility, stealth, and other performance parameters compared with existing U.S. F-16s and F/A-18s or even upgraded versions of these aircraft. A senior Air Force official explicitly stated that the EF-2000 and the Rafale "are in the F-15 class or better."[7] Thus, they argue, without the F-22 U.S. forces could someday have to confront an opponent who, through the purchase of the new European aircraft, possesses major weapon systems equal or superior to those deployed by the American armed forces.[8]

Several questions naturally arise from this defense of the F-22. How real is the "gray threat" posed by the new European fighters? Are public expressions of concern by U.S. Air Force officials and others merely part of the hyperbole of the Washington "budget wars" intended to help protect a favored Air Force procurement program? Or does the "gray threat" raise a potentially important policy issue that deserves serious consideration by defense analysts?

In mid-1994, a RAND research team conducted an extensive series of unclassified interviews with key European government and industry

---

[5]EF-2000, formerly EFA (European Fighter Aircraft), is being developed collaboratively by the United Kingdom, Germany, Italy, and Spain.

[6]*Aerospace Daily*, March 28, 1994. Although rarely mentioned as "gray threats," several other potentially highly capable fighters under development by foreign countries could eventually be exported. Japan is well along in its effort to develop a heavily modified version of the Lockheed F-16 in collaboration with the United States. The Japanese Defense Agency is considering launching development of an all-new Japanese fighter that would be similar in capabilities to the F-22 (see "Japan Launches Quest for Next-Generation Fighter," *Flight International*, 11 October 1994, p. 12). China, Taiwan, and India are also developing new fighters.

[7]Quoted in Jason Glashow and Theresa Hitchens, "DoD Panel to Question Need for F-22 Fighter," *Defense News*, August 22–28, 1994.

[8]For example, see *Aerospace Daily*, February 14, 1994; "Despite End of Cold War, Threats Facing F-22 Are Multiplying," *Aerospace Daily*, November 8, 1993.

officials involved in the development of these fighters.[9] The RAND team hoped to learn more about the new fighters to gain a better understanding of military aerospace technology trends and the management of military R&D in Europe. Specific areas of interest also included European experiences with collaborative R&D, the management of large consortia, translation of military requirements into technical requirements, and transnational technology-sharing. Insights gained from these interviews and research were intended to help U.S. defense planners identify areas for possible future transatlantic technology collaboration, as well as to contribute to a broader understanding of the capabilities of the European aircraft as potential parts of an allied air effort in some future scenario. Although the alleged "gray threat" posed by the European fighters was not the primary focus of this research, the information acquired during the RAND interviews illuminated important aspects of the problem. This report contributes to the debate over the F-22 by examining the "gray threat" in greater detail than has been typical in the press, based on the information gathered by the RAND research team and from published open sources.

As a first cut at evaluating the credibility of the arguments regarding the "gray threat," some additional light must be shed on at least three basic questions about the new European fighters:

*   How good are they and how much better can they get?

*   Will R&D be completed and full-scale production launched?

*   Will the fighters be widely exported outside of Europe?

The unavailability of full data and the many uncertainties about future developments make it impossible to arrive at definitive answers to these questions, particularly the first one. A thorough assessment of the relative performance and combat capabilities of the European fighters compared with current U.S. aircraft would have required

---

[9]Mark Lorell, Daniel Raymer, and Michael Kennedy conducted the interviews in late June and early July 1994 at the Ministry of Defence and the Defence Materiel Administration in Stockholm and Saab Military Aircraft in Linköping for the Swedish Gripen; at the Ministry of Defence and Defence Procurement Executive in London, the Defence Research Agency in Farnborough, British Aerospace Defence in Warton, and Deutsche Aerospace in Munich for the EF-2000; and Dassault Aviation and Matra-Hachette in Paris for the Rafale.

gaining access to a significant amount of unavailable foreign classified or proprietary data to support a major air combat simulation and modeling effort. Furthermore, all three of the fighters are still under development, so their final performance capabilities are not known even by the countries and contractors directly involved in R&D. Even if the necessary data had been available, limitations in time and resources would have prevented us from undertaking truly independent and thorough technical evaluations of these fighters.

Although the full answers to these questions will remain uncertain for some time, and will require extensive technical analysis that goes far beyond what we have attempted here, we can better understand what the ultimate answers may be by drawing together as much of the publicly available information as possible and reviewing it in a critical and coherent fashion. We have not verified nor do we endorse as accurate any of the technical information on the European fighters presented here. We compile this information for our readers to suggest that more extensive analysis is warranted and that concerns expressed by the U.S. Air Force and Department of Defense deserve to be taken seriously.

We begin with a technical description and overview of the three fighters. We then review their likely capabilities and combat effectiveness and make comparisons with existing U.S. fighters. However, we have had to rely largely on European contractor-supplied data that may be suspect. Furthermore, we have had to generate our own rough estimates of a variety of basic technical characteristics and performance measures because of lack of data. We then turn to a brief assessment of the political and budgetary outlook in each country as it may affect the full development and procurement of the aircraft. We then briefly discuss each country's export policies, the likely pricing of the fighters compared to U.S. fighters against which they may compete for foreign sales, and the probable non-European market prospects.[10] We finish by revisiting past assertions about the "gray threat" in light of our findings. We conclude the following:

---

[10]We fully recognize that a truly comprehensive evaluation of the gray threat would include an examination of the overall force structure and capabilities of any country likely to acquire the new fighters. A fighter aircraft, like any other major weapon system, is only a part of a larger integrated force structure in a nation's armed forces. The

- With the new fighters, the Europeans appear to be taking a significant step toward closing the traditional performance gap with American fighters. Armed with the appropriate munitions, these fighters and planned upgraded versions are likely to be highly competitive with existing U.S. fighters and future variants, except for the F-22.

- It is probable that all three European fighters will be fully developed and produced in significant numbers.

- Despite high price tags and a constrained global market, the three European fighters have a reasonable prospect of winning significant foreign orders.

---

combat effectiveness of an air force depends on much more than the capabilities of any given weapon system. Command and control assets, logistics and support infrastructure, doctrine and tactics, the quality and training of pilots and other personnel, and a myriad of other factors play critical roles in determining the overall capabilities of any air force. In most instances, however, acquisition of one of the new European fighters by a reasonably competent air force would likely improve its overall capabilities. In many respects, these fighters are likely to be easier to maintain and operate than some older and more unreliable aircraft. Furthermore, with new-generation "fire-and-forget" missiles and other munitions, the relative importance of pilot skill in determining outcomes may decline considerably.

Chapter Two

TECHNICAL OVERVIEW

Britain, Germany, Italy, France, and Sweden all have long and proud histories as developers and producers of first-rank military fighter aircraft. The jet aircraft was invented in Britain and Germany, and France was active in pushing operational fighters into the supersonic regime. All five have, individually or in consortia, produced first-line jet fighters largely comparable in aerodynamic performance to U.S. aircraft of about the same period. Sweden, with more limited resources, has developed a string of successful jet fighters tailored to its unique operational restrictions, and is notable both for early use of canards and for the production of a jet fighter with short takeoff and landing (STOL) capability using thrust reversers. In the past, however, European fighters tended to be smaller, lighter, and less capable in range and payload compared to contemporary American aircraft. Most observers believed European military engine technology lagged behind that of the United States, with European avionics such as fire-control radars and electronic warfare suites falling far short of the cutting-edge developments in North America.

The three new jet fighters now under development in Europe may require a revision of the traditional views about a technology and capability gap with the United States. All are multirole designs featuring cutting-edge technologies including large integral load-bearing composite structures, canard configuration, relaxed stability with fully computerized digital flight controls, some measure of stealth (at least compared to traditional aircraft), and sophisticated pilot displays and controls. All have features and technology applications of interest to U.S. designers and operators.

The following three subsections provide brief technical overviews of each of the fighters.

EF-2000

The EF-2000, previously called EFA (European Fighter Aircraft), is the product of a consortium of British Aerospace, Deutsche Aerospace, Alenia (Italy), and CASA (Spain), with the United Kingdom and Germany providing technological leadership. Under full-scale development since 1988, EF-2000 is a 46,000-lb, single-seat, twin engine STOL multirole fighter, optimized for air superiority with both BVR (beyond visual range) missile capability and close-in combat agility, but also featuring air-to-ground capabilities. See Figure 1. A two-seat combat-capable trainer version is planned for development, as is a special tactical reconnaissance variant for the Royal Air Force.

RAND*MR611-1*

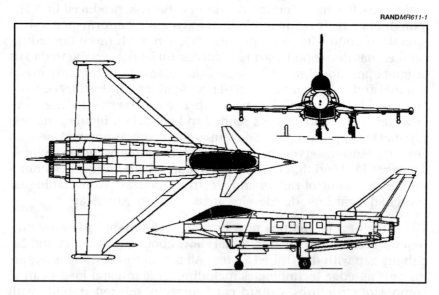

SOURCE: Pilot Press, Ltd.

Figure 1—The Eurofighter EF-2000

EF-2000 first flew in March of 1994. It is an outgrowth of both the British Experimental Aircraft Program (EAP) prototype program and of the Messerschmitt-Bölkow-Blohm (MBB)/Deutsche Aerospace involvement in the X-31 research project and in-house design studies dating back to the early 1980s. It, like the other fighters in this study, is based on the canard/delta wing aerodynamic concept that provides light weight, low supersonic and trim drag, good pitch authority, and substantial fuel volume (although not without certain disadvantages such as a reduced maximum lift coefficient that requires an increased wing area). A fully active, computerized fly-by-wire flight control system coupled with a statically unstable design provide high agility and minimized trim drag. Development of the flight control system has proven to be one of the most difficult aspects of the program, and was the leading cause of the two-year slippage in first flight.

The aircraft has a high concentration of graphite composite construction in the fuselage, wing, and vertical tail, totaling 70 percent of the aircraft structure by weight. The wing and the upper fuselage structures use composite substructure that is cocured, offering less fastener weight and better fuel-sealing. Advanced titanium superplastic forming and diffusion bonding methods are used in fabrication of the canards. Aluminum-lithium is also used. Fuel tanks are made self-sealing with Gortex fibers. A retracting aerial refueling probe is also provided.

Stealth goals established during the design process have been incorporated in a full-scale RCS (radar cross section) test model to verify the design. However, the design shows little indication of the type of stealth-driven geometry seen on such designs as the F-22 and B-2. Stealth features would seem to be limited to absorber materials and coatings, radome and transparency treatments, reduced-emission radar, and inlet and/or engine front face treatments. Such approaches may reduce signature magnitude levels substantially, although operationally significant benefits against advanced threats are likely only from a narrow forward sector.

EF-2000 is designed to use the Eurojet EJ200 engine, a 20,000-lb-class two-shaft advanced afterburning turbofan, featuring reduced maintenance and an increased thrust-to-weight ratio (about 9:1) over the RB199 used on the Panavia Tornado and similar engines. The EJ200, in accelerated ground testing, is being developed by a consortium of Rolls-Royce, MTU-München, FiatAvio, and ITP (Spain). Currently, the two initial EF-2000 prototypes are flying with RB199 engines.

EF-2000 features an advanced avionics suite that includes a new multimode pulse-Doppler look-down/shoot-down radar, a passive infrared search and tracking (IRST) system, a rear-warning radar, jamming electronic countermeasures (ECM), laser warning, missile approach warning, and towed decoys. Fiber-optic data buses are employed. An advanced technology variable-speed constant-frequency generator has encountered some development problems.

The advanced "glass" cockpit features a wide-angle HUD (Head-Up Display), hands-on throttle and stick, a helmet-mounted sight, and voice-activated control. Protection from nuclear, biological, and chemical agents is provided for the pilot, and a liquid conditioning suit keeps the pilot cool.

EF-2000 will normally carry four AIM-120s or other medium-range air-to-air missiles (MRAAMs) in semi-submerged low-drag weapon stores stations, plus two AIM-9 or advanced short-range air-to-air missile (ASRAAMs). A substantial additional load is possible on its 13 external store stations, including a full range of air-to-ground stores and external tanks (three stations are wet). For example, it is possible to simultaneously carry six 1000-lb bombs, four MRAAMs, two ASRAAMs, and a centerline fuel tank. The aircraft is also equipped with a 27-mm Mauser gun.

EF-2000 developers are aiming at a high-reliability goal of nine maintenance man-hours per flight hour (MMH/FH), fully two-thirds less than their figure of 27 MMH/FH for the F/A-18.

RAFALE

Roughly similar to the EF-2000 in size and weight, the Dassault Rafale (Squall) is a 43,000- to 47,000-lb-class, single-seat, twin engine multirole fighter, under development on a purely national basis in France. First flown in 1991, Rafale will be offered in at least three basic versions: the standard single-seat fighter for the French Air Force, a twin-seat, combat-capable trainer variant, and a naval carrier-based version. See Figure 2.

RAND*MR611-2*

NOTE: Side views of air force and naval versions.
SOURCE: Pilot Press, Ltd.

Figure 2—The Dassault Rafale

Rafale is another canard/delta wing design with a fully active, computerized, digital fly-by-wire system and a high percentage of graphite composite construction in the wing and vertical tail. Unlike the EF-2000, which uses an all-composite cocured wing box, the Rafale employs the more conservative technical approach of combining some metal substructure with carbon-fiber composite skins attached with metal fasteners. To reduce development and manufacturing costs, French engineers have cut back on the total amount of composite materials used in the production aircraft compared with the earlier Rafale A prototype technology demonstrator. The canards use advanced titanium superplastic forming/diffusion bonding (selected for cost reasons), and the fuselage has a mixture of graphite composites (25 percent by area) and aluminum-lithium. A detachable aerial refueling probe is available.

Like the EF-2000, Rafale is described as "stealthy," compared to prior designs. But as with the other aircraft in this study, the French fighter's configuration shows little indication of the type of stealth-driven wing and fuselage geometry seen on U.S. designs. However, company literature calls attention to the inlet that is "specially designed for stealthiness purposes." Again, we believe that operationally significant benefits against advanced radar threats are likely only from a narrow forward sector. Company literature also points to infrared (IR) signature reduction via "choice of shapes and materials."

Rafale is equipped with two SNECMA M88-2 engines. This new 16,400-lb-thrust turbofan engine is a two-spool after-burning turbofan that includes improved reliability and maintainability and has no handling restrictions throughout its flight envelope. Advanced technologies employed include digital controls, powder metallurgy, and cooled, microcrystalline vanes.

The new Thomson-CSF/Dassault RBE2 radar has look-down/shoot-down and terrain-following/terrain-avoidance capability. Featuring a two-plane electronically scanned antenna, the RBE2 represents Europe's first electronically scanning phased-array fire-control radar for fighters. An electro-optical (EO)/IRST is provided for passive long-range detection, range-finding, and multitarget tracking. Other avionics include a threat warning radar, electronic countermeasures, IR flares, and a variety of special-purpose pods for laser designation, reconnaissance, and forward-looking infrared (FLIR) operations. The cockpit contains a holographic HUD helmet-mounted sight and multifunction color touch displays. An onboard oxygen generation system (OBOGS) is provided. Electronic hardening protects against electromagnetic pulse (EMP) and lightning.

The navalized carrier version, Rafale M, has been tested at the U.S. Patuxent River Naval Test Center and off the French aircraft carrier *Foch*. This version, limited to 36,376 lb, has 80 percent structure and equipment commonality and 95 percent systems commonality with the land-based Rafale. Major differences include new heavy-duty landing gear, an arresting hook, and some structural reinforcement. A weight increase of only 1300 lb, or 6.5 percent of empty weight, is claimed. However, all Rafale versions have an additional 350-lb structural weight penalty to accommodate the catapult and arresting loads experienced by the navalized variant. The anti-corrosion treatments required for Navy operation are also applied to all Rafales.

Rafale can carry almost 18,000 lb of air-to-air and air-to-ground external stores on 14 store stations, of which five permit over 2200 lb of stores and are wet. For example, it is possible to simultaneously carry 16 500-lb MK82 bombs, two MICA missiles, and two external fuel tanks. In the air-superiority role, Rafale will normally carry up to eight Matra MICA medium-range air-to-air missiles. A DEFA 30-mm cannon is also provided.

Rafale is cleared to 32 degrees angle of attack and has a relatively slow 115-knot approach speed. These features should enhance safety of flight in addition to providing obvious operational benefits.

RAND*MR611-3*

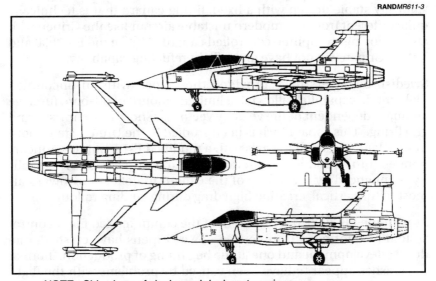

NOTE: Side views of single- and dual-seat versions.
SOURCE: Pilot Press, Ltd.

Figure 3—The Swedish JAS-39 Gripen

GRIPEN

Considerably smaller than either the EF-2000 or the Rafale, the Saab JAS-39 Gripen is an 18,000- to 28,000-lb-class, single-seat, single engine STOL multirole fighter designed for air defense, ground attack, and reconnaissance roles. First flown in 1988, Gripen is designed for the unique Swedish requirement for defensive short-range missions operating from dispersed highway locations. A twin-seat combat-capable trainer version is also being developed, requiring a fuselage stretch and removal of the internal gun.

Like the other two European fighters, Gripen is a canard/delta wing design. Saab has considerable experience with the canard/delta wing configuration, having developed and produced the Viggen STOL fighter beginning in the 1960s. However, the older Viggen is a statically stable design with a fixed, lifting canard that is technically quite different from the modern unstable aircraft like the Gripen with an all-moving, computer-controlled canard. Unlike the EF-2000 and Rafale, Gripen will not have an in-flight refueling capability.

Swedish engineers have provided the Gripen with an uncoupled flight mode capability, allowing a limited amount of off-bore fuselage aiming independent of the velocity vector for short-range missile and gun firing. This capability has been studied in the United States both in simulator tests and in trials with a modified F-16, but never incorporated into a production aircraft. Also, the Gripen's STOL capability is enhanced by the ability of the canard to deflect downward almost to the vertical, creating high drag during landing rollout.

As with the EF-2000, development of the computerized flight control system has not been trouble-free. Two Gripens have crashed, one during development and one at the beginning of production. Both of the crashes appear to have been caused by problems with the flight control system. In the first crash, a developmental prototype went out of control during its sixth flight in February 1989 during final landing approach, and crashed immediately after touchdown. In the second case, a hard pull-up commanded by the pilot during an air show in the summer of 1993 led to divergence in pitch and loss of control of the aircraft. Through changes to the flight control computer software, Saab claims to have eliminated the possibility of a recurrence of the problems that caused these crashes.

Gripen has a high percentage of advanced composite construction in the wing, canard, and vertical tail, totaling 25 percent of the airframe structure. The fuselage is largely of conventional aluminum construction with composite doors and hatches. This more conservative approach to structural materials is believed by many U.S. designers to be superior to an all-composite fuselage, in view of the highly concentrated loads and stresses to which a fighter fuselage is typically subjected.

As with the other aircraft, low RCS is claimed despite little indication of stealth-driven external geometry. The small size of the Gripen probably provides stealth in its own right, which is certainly true for visual detectability. The front of the inlet duct, which is attached last in the production process and was hidden from view of these researchers, is likely made of composite radar-absorbing construction for stealth reasons. It is also possible, although not likely because of performance and icing problems, that some sort of F-117-like screen blockage system is located within the inlet.

The new Swedish fighter is equipped with the 18,000-lb thrust GE/Volvo-Flygmotor F-404-400 engine, a version of the engine used by the U.S. Navy F/A-18 fighter modified to provide greater thrust, improved engine controls, and enhanced bird strike protection. Swedish officials and the Eurojet consortium have recently discussed possible retrofit into the Gripen of the more powerful EJ-200 engine under development for the EF-2000.

The Ericsson PS-05/A multimode pulse-Doppler X-band radar incorporates a mechanically scanned, slotted-wave guide, planar-array antenna and features look-down/shoot-down capability, low probability of intercept (LPI) operation and automatic fire control for guns and missiles. In the air-to-ground mode, the PS-05/A is capable of high-resolution ground mapping. Ground proximity warning, radar warning, and ECM capabilities are provided as well. Also included are provisions for a FLIR/EO pod for air-to-ground combat. The cockpit features a wide-angle HUD and three black-and-white cathode ray tube (CRT) displays.

Gripen will normally carry two AIM-9s on the wing tips, up to four AIM-120s on the wing pylons, and a full range of air-to-ground stores on five external store stations (plus wing-tip AIM-9 rails). A 27-mm

Mauser gun is internally mounted. An additional under-fuselage hard point can carry a sensor or electronic warfare (EW) pod.

An auxiliary power unit (APU) is provided for engine start, alert power, and air conditioning. Gripen is equipped with extensive built-in test capability, and the refuel/rearm combat turnaround time is claimed to be about nine minutes. Total maintenance man-hours per flight hour are put at 12.

Chapter Three

HOW GOOD ARE THE NEW EUROPEAN FIGHTERS?

The preceding technical descriptions indicate that the new European fighters employ a considerable amount of cutting-edge aerospace technology and are likely to be equipped with an impressive array of subsystems and advanced components. Yet the basic question remains: How capable are these weapon systems likely to be when subjected to the ultimate test of aerial combat?

This question is difficult to answer for any new weapon system, even after it is fully developed and tested, and extensive performance and other technical data are made available. Neither of these two conditions apply to the European fighters under consideration here. Nonetheless, we attempt a rough first-order approximation of likely combat capability by developing some basic estimates of air vehicle performance and by examining in greater detail several of the key, high-leverage munitions and subsystems now available or under development for these fighters. In addition, we present some results from European combat simulations, which, while highly suspect in some respects, warrant further examination.

PERFORMANCE ESTIMATES AND COMPARISONS

Table 1 tabulates key design and performance data of interest for the three European fighters. Comparisons are shown for two American fighters: the Lockheed F-16C Block 40, and the McDonnell-Douglas F-15E. We chose the first U.S. aircraft as an example of one of the most advanced operational versions of the standard lightweight multirole fighter that currently predominates in the U.S. Air Force fighter inventory. The F-15E was selected as an example of a high-

Table 1

Technical Comparisons

Parameter	EF-2000	Rafale	Gripen	F-16C-40	F-15E
Maximum weight, lb	46,305	47,400	28,000	42,300	81,000
Design weight,[a] lb	~33,000	~33,500	~20,000	27,185	~49,000
Empty weight, lb	21,495	19,973	14,600	18,238	32,000
Internal fuel, lb	8,818	9,420	5,000	6,846	13,123
Max. ext. load, lb	14,330	17,637	~10,000	12,000	24,500
Store stations, no.	13	14	7	9	11+
Length	52'4"	50'2"	46'3"	49'4"	63'9"
Span	35'11"	35'9"	27'7"	31'0"	42'10"
Wing area, sf	538	495	~330	300	608
Wing loading,[b] psf	61	68	~61	91	81
Max. thrust, lb	40,460	32,800	18,000	23,770	68,200
T/W[b]	1.23	.98	.90	.87	1.39
g limit	9	9	9	9	9
Max. angle of attack	33+	32	26	26	>30
Takeoff distance,[c] ft	970	1,290	1,290	1,400	1,400
Landing distance,[c] ft	1,610	1,290	1,610	2,950	4,250
Maximum speed	M 2.0	M 1.8+	M 2.0	M 2.0+	M 2.5

SOURCES: *Jane's All the World's Aircraft,* company literature, and interviews with European officials.

[a] Estimated takeoff weight; normal air-to-air weapons; no external fuel or conformal fuel tanks (CFTs) (note that F-15E is not normally flown in this configuration).

[b] Based on estimated design weight.

[c] Data for the U.S. aircraft assumes a standard, windless day of 60°F at sea level with design weight for takeoff and 1000 lb remaining fuel for landing; no external tanks or CFTs, maximum afterburner throttle; a standard air-to-air weapons load; and 0 percent slope, dry concrete runway conditions. Assumptions for the European aircraft are unknown.

NOTE: ~ indicates rough guess from available public data.

end strike/attack version of America's most capable air superiority fighter.

Some data in Table 1 are estimated or inferred. All data should be viewed with considerable caution because the use of multiple sources may imply different assumptions, company brochure data may be optimistic, and standard open sources such as *Jane's All the World's Aircraft,* while usually reliable, may contain unknown errors. Mutually consistent range data were not available and so are not provided in Table 1, although such data would be of great interest. However, it would appear that the EF-2000 and Rafale probably have ranges somewhat greater than the F-16, and the Gripen somewhat less. The F-15E is probably superior to all as a result of its massive fuel load.

The published absolute maximum takeoff gross weight is a misleading parameter for comparison of maneuvering potential because it simply measures how many external stores and tanks can be attached before the landing gear is overstressed. A "combat weight" should be used instead. In the absence of such data, air combat takeoff weight was approximated in Table 1 as the empty weight plus internal fuel, air-to-air weapons, and estimated miscellaneous useful load (ammunition, flares, crew, etc.). External tanks were assumed to have been dropped, if used at all. This weight was used to determine the thrust-to-weight ratio (T/W) and wingloading (W/S) to provide a measure of performance comparison (high T/W and low W/S imply good combat maneuverability in most cases).

As can be seen, these European aircraft are impressive in many respects. The EF-2000 and Rafale are quite similar in several parameters, including gross weight, payload weight, number of store stations, physical dimensions, speed, and field lengths. EF-2000 shows an advantage in terms of T/W, a key measure in close-in dogfighting.

Our estimates of the basic performance data relevant to aerial combat for the EF-2000 and Rafale indicate a clear superiority over the F-16C Block 40, and essential equivalence in important areas with the F-15E. Since it is a much smaller fighter, the Gripen is not surprisingly outclassed by the F-15 as well as by the other two European fighters. Nonetheless, the lightweight Swedish entry compares favorably in several respects with the F-16. All three fighters show a superior T/W compared with the F-16, whereas the EF-2000 is close to the F-15E. The two larger European fighters boast angle-of-attack (AOA) capabilities superior or roughly comparable to the American fighters'. Gripen's AOA is probably about the same as the F-16's. These data do not reflect important agility advantages that all three European fighters may possess because of the static instability of their basic designs and their canard/delta configurations, combined with their advanced fly-by-wire flight control systems. Indeed, Gripen may actually perform much better in actual aerial combat than suggested by these data because of its uncoupled flight mode capabilities.

The new European fighters appear to have a more than adequate air-to-ground capability. Although none of the European fighters is primarily oriented toward ground-attack operations, EF-2000 and Rafale are nonetheless are expected to carry a significant quantity and variety of stores. These two fighters appear to be superior in these areas compared with published numbers for the F-16. Maximum external loads for the Rafale surpass 70 percent of the capability of the much larger F-15E strike/fighter.

Even assuming the data presented in Table 1 are largely accurate, they still provide only the barest hint of the likely future combat potential of the European fighters. Without a full-scale air-to-air combat simulation analysis, it is difficult to assess who the winner might be in any potential combat between current U.S. fighters and "gray threat" aircraft such as these. Much depends upon the relative missile, radar, and overall signature features of the warring aircraft, as well as a host of other variables for which data are not available.

Nonetheless, additional insights into various aspects of the likely combat capabilities of the European fighters and their future variants can be gleaned through a closer examination of several other factors. These include:

- New-generation subsystems and munitions of particular interest
- European combat assessments and simulations
- Planned upgrades and future technology developments.

NEW-GENERATION SUBSYSTEMS AND MUNITIONS

As noted in Chapter Two, European planners intend to develop and equip their new fighters with a variety of high-leverage advanced subsystems and munitions. Several of these have high potential for enhancing the fighters' combat effectiveness in ways that cannot be captured by comparisons of basic airframe/engine performance data.

Subsystems of particular interest include the RBE2 fire-control radar intended for the Rafale, and the integrated electronic warfare systems (IEWS) and IRST systems under development for EF-2000 and Rafale. Not only do these systems exhibit many cutting-edge technologies and capabilities, they point to a potentially significant narrowing of the historical gap between American and European military avionics.

The RBE2 is Europe's first phased-array fire-control radar intended for a fighter. This type of radar can provide major operational advantages over existing radars. Conventional radars employ the familiar antenna dishes or arrays mounted on gimbals that, powered by electric or hydraulic motors, mechanically scan the horizon. These are the types of radars deployed on current U.S. combat fighter aircraft such as the F-15 and F-16. Phased-array radars replace the mechanically scanned antenna dish with a fixed array of hundreds of individual ports for transmitting and receiving microwave energy, and employ electronic phase-shifting beam steering in place of mechanical scanning. Phased-array radars can dramatically reduce radar cross section (providing greater stealthiness), increase simultaneous multiple target engagement capabilities, extend target detection range, enhance survivability and reliability, and reduce the weight and size of the overall subsystem.[1] French contractors claim that the RBE2 can detect and track targets out to the maximum effective range of all existing American and French medium-range air-to-air missiles.

No current U.S. fighter is equipped with a phased-array radar, although an active phased-array system is under development for the F-22. The Westinghouse/Texas Instruments APG-77 is likely to far surpass the overall capabilities of the Rafale's RBE2, in part because the American radar is based on more-advanced technology. The APG-77's fixed antenna is made up of large numbers of individual solid-state transmitting and receiving (T/R) modules based on gallium-arsenide monolithic microwave integrated circuit (MMIC) technology, which significantly increases efficiency, power output, and survivability compared with passive systems such as the RBE2.[2] Nonetheless, the French system represents a major technological advance over conventional technology in existing U.S. fighters. And

---

[1]See General Research Corporation, *Strategic Industrial Initiative: Phased Array Radar Study*, Fairborn, Ohio, June 1990, pp. 2-1 to 2-6.

[2]The RBE2 is a "passive" phased-array radar, which means it has only a single source of microwave energy. Each of the hundreds of T/R modules on the F-22 radar array has its own source of microwave energy, providing greater performance capability, more graceful degradation, and enhanced survivability.

although some developmental problems and delays have been experienced, the French radar appears to be well along in the R&D process.

Other avionics of note include the IEWS and IRST systems under development for the EF-2000 and Rafale. Historically, European contractors have lagged considerably behind the United States in the development of electronic warfare systems, which are so important for survival and combat success in modern aerial combat. In the past, European air forces often have used externally mounted American EW pods or other lower-capability domestic products. No European fighter has ever been equipped with a fully integrated internal EW system.

This situation will be changed by the Defensive Aids Sub-System (DASS) under development for the EF-2000 by the Eurodass consortium headed by GEC Marconi Defence Systems in the United Kingdom and Elctronica in Italy,[3] and the IEWS planned for the Rafale. No one knows how well these systems will perform once full development is completed. However, according to detailed combat simulation studies conducted by the British Defence Research Agency (DRA) and reported to the House of Commons in May 1994, DASS is a critical subsystem that adds considerably to the overall combat effectiveness of EF-2000.[4]

Both EF-2000 and Rafale will be equipped with new-technology IRST systems. These systems will provide a passive option for locating and tracking aerial targets. Because they do not emit energy as do fire-control radars that can give away a fighter's location to the enemy, they increase stealthiness. They also could provide a means (under certain circumstances) of tracking fighters with low radar cross section by detecting heat caused by the engine and the friction of high-speed flight. Simulations conducted by the British DRA show that IRST adds substantially to EF-2000's combat effectiveness.[5]

---

[3]Currently the DASS is scheduled for use in only the British and Italian versions of the EF-2000.

[4]See House of Commons, Defence Committee, *Progress on the Eurofighter 2000 Programme*, London, Her Majesty's Stationery Office, 4 May 1994, pp. 29–30.

[5]Some Russian fighters are also equipped with IRST systems.

All three fighters are equipped with many other interesting and potentially effective subsystems and components. However, nothing is
more important for the future capabilities of these fighters than the
new air-to-air missiles that are currently planned or under development. Combat simulation studies conducted by RAND and others
have suggested that new-generation, high-capability air-to-air missiles can provide a decisive edge in air combat. Most important
among these missiles are the new "fire-and-forget" weapons that use
active autonomous radar seekers for long range, and new-generation
all-aspect imaging infrared (IIR) seekers for close-in combat. These
missiles are so capable that they reduce the relative importance for
combat outcomes of pilot skill and the flight performance capabilities of the launch platform.

The only operational Western BVR missile in this class is the
American AIM-120 Advanced Medium-Range Air-to-Air Missile
(AMRAAM). The U.S. government carefully controls export of this
missile because of proliferation concerns. However, existing or
planned European missiles intended for the new fighters may be able
to roughly equal or even surpass the capabilities of AMRAAM,
particularly early versions.

Rafale is designed to use the Matra-Hachette MICA air-to-air missile,
a weapon similar in many respects to the AMRAAM. Unlike
AMRAAM, MICA will be available in both active radar and IIR-guided
variants.[6] Both can be used for either short- or medium-range combat. Rafale can carry both types simultaneously, giving the pilot
greater options in a heavily jammed combat environment. French
contractors claim MICA weighs about one-quarter less than
AMRAAM and, with an effective maximum range of about 60 miles, is
roughly equivalent to the American missile.[7] They insist that it actually performs better at close range than AMRAAM, and that MICA's
smaller warhead has a larger lethality zone.

---

[6]Development of the IIR version is slated for completion two years after the radar
variant. The active radar version of MICA is in production but is not yet fully operational. About 80 of a planned 100 test firings have been completed.

[7]In most realistic operational scenarios, the effective range would be considerably
less. The IIR version of MICA has about 10 percent less range than the radar version
because of the different seeker heads.

The radar version of MICA has an active seeker with midcourse update, and uses hardened commercial processors for cost savings. The IIR version's seeker is all-aspect. MICA features both aerodynamic control fins and thrust vectoring via tiny vanes in the motor exhaust, and is capable of extreme off-boresight launch using Rafale's helmet-mounted sight. Also, MICA can be either rail-launched or ejected.

French industry, in collaboration with British firms, is also examining upgraded variants of MICA with longer range and much higher speed. The purpose of these improvements is to increase the enemy "no-escape zone" and improve prospects against low-RCS targets by raising mean velocity. According to Matra, MICA has greater growth potential than AMRAAM. Because the French missile was developed five years after AMRAAM, Matra claims that its electronics are more integrated, weigh less, and take up less space. This permits the addition of more propellant for higher speed and greater range.

A more radical option under serious consideration is to retrofit a solid-fuel ramjet. Contractor studies suggest this would add no additional weight and increase the "no-escape zone" by three times over the existing MICA or AMRAAM. The ramjet MICA would have an effective range of about 90 miles. This missile would begin entering service about 2005.[8]

The British Procurement Executive and the Royal Air Force (RAF) are currently examining options to fulfill a requirement for a future medium-range air-to-air missile (FMRAAM) (Air Staff Requirement [ASR] 1239) for EF-2000. British officials are seeking a missile with longer range, higher speed, and greater agility in the final combat phase than that possessed by the existing AIM-120 AMRAAM, to help counter more-stealthy future threat fighters.

---

[8]The electronic counter-countermeasures (ECCM) capabilities of the MICA and other new European missiles are unknown. ECCM capability will likely be a critical factor for advanced missiles in future combat scenarios. Most European contractor discussions of the U.S. AIM-120 AMRAAM appear to refer to the "A" version. The United States is also considering the possibility of adding a ramjet capability to extend the range of future AMRAAM versions.

FMRAAM could be an upgraded AMRAAM—providing British industry won a major role in joint R&D—or an all-European missile. However, Matra-Hachette and British Aerospace Dynamics are likely to complete a merger on a 50-50 basis by the end of the year, which will probably greatly increase the chances for an all-European FMRAAM for EF-2000.[9] The extensive Matra studies on upgrading MICA are clearly aimed at fulfilling the FMRAAM requirement. In exchange for developing a new long-range high-energy FMRAAM based on MICA technology, the French may procure some ASRAAM (advanced short-range air-to-air missiles) developed by British industry for use on the Rafale.

Thus, in all likelihood, the Rafale and EF-2000 will eventually be equipped with highly capable all-European missiles that may equal or surpass in some respects the U.S. AMRAAM. Although Matra heavily marketed the MICA for use on the Gripen, the Swedish government recently confirmed its decision to buy the AIM-120 AMRAAM. However, the size of the Swedish buy was lower than expected. Some observers have speculated that this purchase is seen as a gap-filler for the initial operational Gripens as they begin to enter service with the Swedish Air Force. Later, they argue, the movement toward greater European integration and other factors will push Sweden toward adoption of a European FMRAAM or some upgraded version of MICA.

As the preceding discussion has indicated, the European air forces and contractors place a great deal of emphasis on the BVR combat regime. Despite the likelihood that most future engagements will be fought in this fashion, air-to-air warfare will to some degree still take place with the combatants within visual range (WVR) of each other, including the classic close-in dogfight.[10] Aircraft maneuverability and energy considerations play the dominant role in such engagements and will remain an important aspect. We have already noted the agility of the advanced European fighters in this regard.

---

[9]May 1995 information indicates that the merger has not been completed. However, according to a March 1995 article from *Defense Daily*, the missile merger negotiations are "proceeding well and a large number of major issues have been resolved." The article also notes that the combined company would have sales of $1 billion.

[10]This discussion on advanced short-range air-to-air missiles was provided by Major Arthur Huber (USAF), an Air Force Fellow at RAND.

However, the capabilities of new short-range air-to-air missiles under development by the Europeans and others promise to significantly alter the way dogfighting will be conducted in the future. Advanced missiles in this class are under development in Britain and France, as well as in Russia, Japan, and Israel. Apparently, many if not all of these countries will make these lethal products available on the international market.

The most important foreign missiles in this class include the ASRAAM (UK), MICASRAAM (France), Archer (Russia), Python 4 (Israel), and the AAM-4/5 (Japan). These missiles possess advanced IR or imaging IR sensors and deliver superior IR counter-countermeasures (IRCCM) performance. In many cases, the seekers in these missiles can be operated at high off-boresight axis angles that allow shots in situations previously considered impossible. A cueing system allows the pilot to designate the target at high angles off the nose of the aircraft and outside the field-of-view of the HUD. In the MiG-29 armed with the Archer missile, this is accomplished by a helmet-mounted sight. The French and British are both developing similar cueing systems. With their increased range, outstanding agility, and robust IRCCM, these new missiles, coupled with highly agile launch platforms such as the new European fighters, could be good enough that the first shot will lead invariably to the first kill.

Although air-to-air capabilities have been a primary concern in the new fighter development, the Europeans are also planning on procuring significant new-technology air-to-ground munitions. The French contractors Matra and Aerospatiale have been particularly active in this area. The powered Matra Apache stand-off munitions dispenser is planned for service entry in the late 1990s. This dispenser will carry smart submunitions for attacking high-value fixed targets, runways, and armor. Matra is also conducting developmental studies for a new stealthy air-launched long-range cruise missile called the HPTGD (*Haute Précision Très Grande Distance* [Long-range high-precision cruise missile]). This missile would be based on the Apache and have a range up to 360 miles. Aerospatiale is also proposing a similar missile based on its ASMP (*Air-Sol Moyenne Porté* [Medium-range air-to-surface missile]), which is already in service with the French Air Force. Apache will probably be procured by the German air force, since the missile has become a cooperative venture with Deutsche Aerospace.

The RAF is seeking to fulfill a requirement (ASR 1236) for a conventionally armed nonstealthy stand-off missile (CASOM) with a range of about 150 miles, and a modern anti-armor weapon (ASR 1238). With the Matra–British Aerospace (BAe) deal, ASR 1236 could be filled by a version of Apache.

Gripen will be equipped with a new German-developed stand-off glide-bomb dispenser called the DWS39. The Swedish fighter will also carry Maverick and the Saab Rb15 anti-ship missile.

EUROPEAN COMBAT SIMULATIONS AND ASSESSMENTS

European contractors and government agencies have conducted numerous computer combat simulations and other combat assessments of their aircraft. While they must be viewed with a great deal of skepticism, several were clearly conducted with a high level of professionalism and sophistication, and are worth reviewing. Analysts may dispute specific assumptions and outcomes of these simulations, but they can not be dismissed as entirely without merit, particularly those simulations conducted by government agencies such as the DRA in Britain.

In 1993 and 1994, BAe and the DRA conducted an extensive series of computer combat simulations to examine the combat effectiveness of various versions of EF-2000 and compare the Eurofighter to future Russian aircraft as well as other fighters. Both studies focused on beyond visual range air-to-air combat and assumed a threat aircraft with the capabilities of an upgraded Russian Su-27 (Su-35) equipped with an AMRAAM-like missile. DRA's simulations appear to have been considerably more sophisticated than BAe's, which apparently were limited to small engagements of 2 v 2 (two fighters versus two fighters) or smaller, whereas DRA went as high as 8 v 8. DRA used its special Air Combat Simulation Facility, which houses the JOUST computer model. JOUST is an impressive "pilot-in-the-loop" simulation that permits up to eight pilots to simultaneously "fly" against each other in large-scale simulated BVR and close-in combat engagements.

Both studies used an overall effectiveness outcome scale that ranks fighters from 0 to 1.0. The higher the number earned by a given fighter, the greater the probability that the fighter wins in a specific mission. Thus, a score of 0 means the fighter will always lose, whereas a score of 1.0 means it will always win. A score of .5 means a fighter will experience a 1:1 exchange ratio. Some of the results of these simulations are shown in Table 2, along with our calculations of how the scores translate into more traditional exchange ratios (enemy lost to friendly lost).

The scores from both studies indicate that the EF-2000 is superior to all fighters examined with the exception of the F-22. Furthermore, BAe proudly points out that the F-22 is only about 10 percent higher on their effectiveness scale but costs about twice as much as the Eurofighter. However, when translated into exchange ratios—the more traditional way of measuring combat effectiveness—the F-22 comes out looking much better, with over double the effectiveness of the EF-2000. All existing U.S. fighters with the exception of the F-15 are claimed to have performed relatively poorly in these simulations. Even the F-15 is shown as barely exceeding a 1:1 exchange ratio, and is placed well below the EF-2000. Although Rafale does not do particularly well, it is shown as competitive with the F-15 and superior to other U.S. fighters. Gripen does not fare as well as the other new

Table 2

Combat Simulation Scores Claimed by British Industry and Government

Fighter	British Aerospace		Defence Research Agency	
	Effectiveness Score	Inferred Exchange Ratio[a]	Effectiveness Score[b]	Inferred Exchange Ratio[a]
F-22	.91	10:1	.90	9:1
EF-2000	.82	4.5:1	.75	3:1
F-15F	.60	1.5:1		
F-15E			.55	1.2:1
Rafale	.50	1:1	.50	1:1
F-15C	.43	1:1.3		
F-18E/F	.25	1:3	.45	1:1.2
F-18C	.21	1:3.8		
F-16C	.21	1:3.8		
Gripen			.40	1:1.5
Mirage 2000			.35	1:1.8
Tornado F.3			.30	1:2.3

SOURCE: British Aerospace and Defence Research Agency.

[a]Assumed exchange ratio (enemy to friendly killed) inferred from effectiveness scores.

[b]Approximate values.

European fighters, in part because of its limitations in radar range, speed, and acceleration. However, the DRA claims that it performed about as well as the F-18E/F, the heavily modified and upgraded version of the Hornet under development by McDonnell-Douglas.[11]

Because most of the assumptions and data used by the British are not known, we cannot assess the validity of these findings. Given the strong incentives for having the EF-2000 perform well, considerable skepticism is warranted.[12]   Nonetheless, we would be hesitant to dismiss these findings out of hand. DRA is a highly professional civilian government organization, and is certainly not controlled by the RAF or British contractors.

Indeed, some of the general insights DRA gained from the simulations appear informative. According to DRA, the simulations show the great importance of high-energy agility and maneuverability even in BVR engagements. Perhaps most interesting, they indicate the enormous advantages provided by low radar cross section and stealthiness in general. The only feasible way to try to counter stealth, representatives told us, is to procure a very high speed, extremely agile long-range missile and to employ third-party targeting. These outcomes led to the formulation of the FMRAAM requirement and Matra's plans for upgrading MICA. The F-22, of course, is the only fighter in the simulations that was designed from its inception with full stealth features.

Not surprisingly, the French are less than ecstatic about the outcomes of the British simulations, although they agree about the importance of FMRAAM. Matra and Dassault have conducted many of their own combat simulations, including real-time man-in-the-loop simulations similar to DRA's. One large-scale effort was conducted at the German government IABG facility near Munich, using the SILKA simulation. These simulations included 4 v 12 scenarios, where four friendly fighters were trying to shoot down eight enemy

---

[11]Again, these simulation results must be treated with extreme caution. For example, the fact that the BAe results indicate only a relatively small improvement in capability provided by the nearly all-new F-18E/F compared with the existing F/A-18C seems highly suspect.

[12]At least some of these simulations were conducted at a time when Parliament was reassessing the overall cost-effectiveness of the EF-2000 program and considering radical options for reducing costs.

bombers escorted by four fighters. The enemy fighters were MiG-29s and Su-27s armed with AA-11 missiles. Friendly fighters possessed MICA, AMRAAM, and other missiles. BVR combat started about 60 miles out. Different friendly fighters were modeled using the same missiles.

Matra claims that, using the British effectiveness score, Rafale scored between .8 and nearly 1.0, depending on assumptions. Furthermore, the French insist that using similar scenario assumptions, tactics, equipment, and munitions, Rafale performs roughly the same as EF-2000. Matra claims that differing assumptions about onboard equipment and intelligence capabilities make a large difference. For example, if any of the fighters is equipped with a "pilot assistant," or can detect departure of the enemy missiles, performance is greatly improved.

Like British officials, Matra representatives argue that Gripen suffers from insufficient high-energy maneuvering capabilities. However, Saab offers several counterarguments. Swedish officials maintain that analysts should look at overall fighter force capability over an air campaign, not merely the combat performance of platforms in specific engagements. They argue that Gripen will permit a much higher sortie rate and far greater basing flexibility than typical fighters, because of its rapid combat turnaround capability, STOL attributes, and its ability to operate from dispersed road sites with small ground crews and little support equipment. Government tests have demonstrated a 10-minute turnaround rate using a standard ground crew of one technician and five conscripts. The test included refueling and rearming with air-to-ground munitions, missiles, and gun ammunition. Thus, a high sortie rate can generate a much higher overall force effectiveness (assuming a sufficient number of aircraft can survive combat). The Swedes insist that new-generation BVR missiles used in conjunction with a ground air defense radar net and combined with Gripen's small signature and rapid turnaround rates will make the fighter an effective weapon system.

In short, all three of the new European fighters appear to possess some impressive capabilities. Whatever the real capabilities of their fighters, the European developers seem to be narrowing the historical performance gap between European and American fighters, at least when the F-22 is removed from the comparison. Furthermore, the Europeans are not standing still—they continue to examine new technologies and concepts to upgrade their fighters.

PLANNED UPGRADES AND FUTURE TECHNOLOGY DEVELOPMENTS

While admitting that Gripen does not match the performance of the other two European fighters, Swedish officials point out that both government and industry are examining major upgrade programs to take place around 2001. The two highest-priority areas under consideration are information systems and air vehicle performance. The first area would seek to upgrade avionics and sensors, particularly the radar and onboard computers. The second would focus on enhancing speed and kinetic energy for agility and maneuvering, as well as increasing range and reducing signature. Options under consideration include installation of a more powerful engine such as the EJ200 and a new wing design. The major consideration is to enhance Gripen's capabilities to take the most advantage possible of next-generation long-range BVR missiles. A new two-seat version of Gripen already under development could be modified into a new attack version at some later date.

Current and past technology studies in the United Kingdom and Germany go far beyond these considerations. Contractors in both countries are looking at new fighter technology concepts that could also contribute to later upgrades of the EF-2000. These studies focus heavily on stealth, particularly reducing RCS.

BAe is undertaking a prefeasibility study of future offensive aircraft (FOA) to replace Tornado GR.1/GR.4s after 2015. The company has invested a considerable amount of money into a new facility for developing stealth technologies and concepts. BAe is also looking at next-generation aircraft (NGA) for an EF-2000 follow-on. In addition to stealth technologies and designs, BAe engineers are examining areas such as "smart" skins and structures, advanced avionics architectures, and system design processes.

Deutsche Aerospace has completed several extensive studies of low-RCS technologies and designs. The Lampyridae (Fire Fly) study, was launched in 1981 with the goal of producing a low-RCS fighter design. The resulting design, which resembles the Lockheed F-117 stealth fighter, was built as a three-quarter-scale model and extensively "flown" by a pilot while tethered in a wind tunnel. Technicians also built a full-scale model about 40 feet long to test for RCS signature. While radar-absorbing materials (RAM) were used in the inlet areas, most of the low RCS was achieved through fuselage shaping similar to the F-117's. Deutsche Aerospace officials claimed that U.S. designs such as the F-117, B-2, and YF-22 were also tested, and the Lampyridae proved more effective than the first American aircraft. This program ended in 1987.

Deutsche Aerospace is now attempting to launch a new program for full flight test demonstration to further advance its earlier stealth research, as well as integrated flight and propulsion controls, modular avionics, and pilot assistants. It is hoped that the new program, called CATD (Combat Aircraft Technology Demonstrator), will become a European collaborative effort. A major focus will be to reduce radar, IR, and acoustic signatures, as well as to develop and integrate new sensors and avionics. The program's goal is to ultimately develop a new fighter with an initial operational capability in 2020.

Another area of advanced technology being strongly pushed by the Germans is "super maneuverability," which they argue provides dramatic advantages in aerial combat. Since the very earliest discussions in the 1970s over a future European fighter, German engineers led by the late Wolfgang Herbst argued for the development of "post-stall" maneuvering capabilities to permit radically increased agility in air combat. Although the Germans were unable to convince their European partners to include these capabilities in the EF-2000, Deutsche Aerospace went ahead to develop and test the necessary thrust-vectoring technologies with the X-31 program, a collaborative U.S.-German effort. The company still hopes to incorporate thrust vectoring on later versions of the EF-2000. Several U.S. test programs have also examined these technologies. Although the F-22 will be equipped with two-dimensional thrust vectoring, no currently deployed U.S. fighter possesses "super maneuverability."

Whether or not the British and German technology programs, and similar French efforts, lead to an all-new fighter in the foreseeable future, they are likely to produce new technologies and concepts that can be applied to upgraded versions of their current new fighters.

With so much emphasis being placed on stealth and signature reduction, new avionics, and enhanced maneuverability, it is possible that the current fighters will ultimately reflect these improvements, significantly increasing their overall combat performance.

CONCLUDING OBSERVATIONS ON PERFORMANCE COMPARISONS

Based on our comparisons of basic performance data, the British simulation results, and a variety of other factors, it seems likely that the F-22 would perform effectively against any of the European fighters in beyond-visual-range combat as a result of its stealth, super cruise, and radar capabilities. If a "leaker"[13] ever managed to get within close-in/visual combat range, the F-22 would in all probability match or best the opposition because of its high agility, high excess power (thrust minus drag), and pilot-friendly avionics, controls, and displays. However, almost any future aircraft with a highly agile, high off-boresite missile would be a potent threat even to the F-22 in close-in combat.

The F-15 or F-16 would likely be a more even match, especially against EF-2000 and Rafale. Without substantial modifications, these older U.S. aircraft probably have higher signatures, rough equivalence or worse radar and missile performance, and no clear performance advantage for close-in combat. Gripen, if it can get to close-in combat, would also likely be a real threat, but in BVR combat its small radar aperture would probably limit its effectiveness.

We do not suggest that current U.S. aircraft would be outclassed by these fighters in air combat, despite the European simulation results, but U.S. forces might be confronted with a rough parity in exchange ratios. Many would argue that such an outcome, in some future "Desert Storm" against an opponent who has purchased a number of these European fighters, would be politically unacceptable.

Further, the Europeans can be expected to upgrade and improve the new fighters as they continue to enter service, particularly in regard to stealth, avionics, and munitions. There also is a distinct possibil-

---

[13]A "leaker" is a plane that makes it through the long-range defensive perimeter.

ity, based on the technology programs under way in Europe, that a new, very low RCS fighter could be developed in the next decade or two.

However, it is important to remember that capable as the European fighters may be on a technical and performance level, they pose no threat at all if they never complete development and are never procured. All three of the programs discussed above have been the subject of considerable political controversy at many times during their development; indeed, the EF-2000 has been confidently pronounced dead on more than one occasion. The Eurofighter is in a particularly difficult political situation again in Germany. Are these fighters likely to survive the political and budgetary controversies that surround them, or will they eventually be canceled as relics of the Cold War? It is to these questions that we now turn.

Chapter Four

WILL R&D BE COMPLETED AND PRODUCTION LAUNCHED?

This chapter briefly assesses the current status and political outlook of each of the three programs. These assessments assume that no major crisis will profoundly change the geopolitical situation in each of the participating countries.

JAS-39 GRIPEN: PRODUCTION IS WELL UNDER WAY

The Gripen program has caused considerable controversy in Sweden, dating back to the late 1970s when left-wing parties strongly opposed the development of a new fighter. Since then, cost growth and technical problems have continued to disrupt the program. Nonetheless, Gripen has now entered into full production, and is almost certain to be procured in significant numbers by the Swedish air force (SAF).

Two highly publicized crashes during R&D seriously jeopardized the program. As mentioned earlier, the first developmental prototype crashed in February 1989 only a few months after its maiden flight, because of problems with the flight control system. This accident, plus escalating costs, threatened negotiations between the government and industry for the first major production batch of 110 fighters, which was planned to follow the initial production run of 30 aircraft ordered in 1982. The program was delayed while contractors rewrote major portions of the flight control computer software, and while the Swedish parliament carefully scrutinized technical and financial problems.

Industry eventually convinced the government that the technical difficulties had been corrected, and a new price was settled on for the first large production batch. In 1992, the SAF placed its order for the production lot of 110 JAS-39s. Unfortunately, in August 1993, the first completed production Gripen suffered a spectacular loss of control over Stockholm during an air show and crashed into an uninhabited island, while tens of thousands of horrified spectators looked on.[1]

The Swedish parliament, still investigating cost growth and technical problems ensuing from the first crash, virtually halted the program after the embarrassing setback over the capital city. Parliament established a special all-party commission to fully investigate the second crash. This commission later broadened its charter to include a full review of the entire program, with the objective of making a final decision on whether to proceed with full production.

After a thorough and extensive five-month investigation, the commission sent its eagerly awaited final report to Defense Minister Anders Bjorck in January 1994. To the relief of industry, the report cleared the way for final full development and production of the Gripen. After carefully reviewing all technical aspects of the R&D effort, the commission concluded that "the JAS project can be expected to achieve the goals set up by the government in **all** significant respects."[2] The flight control system, thought to be cause of both crashes, had come under particularly close scrutiny. The commission considered "appropriate" the safeguards that IG JAS (Industry Group Jakt [fighter], Attack [attack], Spaning [reconnaissance]) and FMV (Försvarets Materielverk [Defense Materiel Administration]) put into place to "strengthen their capability in the flight control system."[3]

Although the two accidents and investigations had caused about a year's delay, the final parliamentary report cleared the way for final

---

[1]The same pilot was at the controls during both crashes. He survived. No one on the ground was killed or injured.

[2]See Johan Rapp and Charles Bickers, "Crash commission green lights Gripen," *Jane's Defence Weekly*, International Edition, January 22, 1994, p. 19. Emphasis added.

[3]Ibid.

development and full production.[4] The Defense Minister was upbeat after reviewing the report, noting that: "After the thorough study it has been subjected to, I find that the project is on firm ground."[5] Indeed it is. As of December 1993, the five prototypes had completed 1204 test flights.[6] Ten fighters were slated for delivery during 1994 to the Swedish Defense Materiel Administration. The remaining 30 aircraft of the first production series are slated for delivery by the beginning of 1996.[7] In the summer of 1994, some 20 Gripens could be seen in various stages of final assembly at Saab's facilities in Linköping. Current plans call for the manufacture and delivery of the main production batch of 110 aircraft at a yearly rate of about 20, with final delivery in 2002. In the late 1990s, the government will decide on a second major production batch, so that the SAF can replace all of its Viggens and Drakens with the new fighter as originally envisioned. A total production run of around 300 Gripens for the SAF is hoped for.

The government authorized 14 examples of a significant new version to be included in the second production batch, the JAS-39B, a two-seater with an all-new forward fuselage.[8] Delivery of the JAS-39B will begin in 1998. The two-seat Gripen could ultimately be upgraded into a specialized ground-attack variant.

In sum, there is virtually no doubt that the JAS-39 will be fully developed and at least 140 will be procured by the SAF. Barring new major technical problems, it seems likely the government will also approve another major production batch in the late 1990s to complete SAF modernization plans and maintain the Swedish military aerospace industrial base.

---

[4]Each accident resulted in about half a year of delay, according to officials at Saab-Scania.

[5]Johan Rapp and Charles Bickers, op. cit.

[6]See *Aerospace Daily*, December 12, 1993, p. 502.

[7]See *Aerospace Daily*, ibid., and "Industrigruppen JAS to Resume Deliveries of JAS 39 Gripen," *Dagens Industri*, April 22, 1994.

[8]See Theresa Hitchens, "Sweden Pushes Two-Seat Gripen," *Defense News*, January 27, 1992, pp. 16, 18, and Julian Moxon, "SAAB Reshuffle Aims at Gripen Exports," *Flight International*, February 5, 1995, p. 16.

RAFALE: STEADY AND ON COURSE

Throughout its history, Rafale has generated far less political contro-versy than EF-2000 or Gripen. No highly publicized major technical snags have arisen to mar the development effort and fuel criticism of the program. Rafale has experienced some technical difficulties and schedule slippage, and its high costs have caused concern, but the R&D program is now generally viewed as politically secure. As a key program in the new French five-year military budgetary law, the new fighter almost certainly will complete development and enter into series production.

Rafale emerged in the mid-1980s following the French withdrawal from the European effort to launch a collaborative fighter program. The chiefs of staff of France, Germany, Great Britain, Italy, and Spain began official discussions on a new collaborative fighter in October 1982.[9] They agreed over the main characteristics of a common air-craft in December 1983. However, problems soon arose. The French sought design leadership—to avoid the inefficiencies of program management by committees—and selection of a French engine. In addition, the French preferred a considerably lighter aircraft than envisioned by the other partners, in order to keep costs down, satisfy French navy requirements for a carrier-based fighter, and facilitate export sales. Unable to resolve these problems, the French withdrew from the collaborative effort in July 1985. Dassault then moved ahead with an all-French program based on a scaled-down version of the Rafale A technology demonstrator, which first flew in July 1986.[10] Prime Minister Jacques Chirac announced his government's formal "approval of the development of a new fighter to be derived from the Rafale demonstrator" in February 1987.[11]

---

[9]The joint development program was announced by the Panavia consortium, which was composed of British Aerospace (BAe), Messerschmitt-Bölkow-Blohm (MBB), and Aeritalia. See Yolande Simon, *Prospects for the French Fighter Industry in a Post–Cold War Environment: Is the Future More Than a Mirage?* RAND, Dissertation, RGSD-106, 1993, p. 7, for a detailed analysis of the origins of the Rafale program.

[10]See Mark Lorell, *The Use of Prototypes in Selected Foreign Fighter Aircraft Develop-ment Programs: Rafale, EAP, Lavi, and Gripen*, RAND, R-3687-P&L, September 1989.

[11]Ibid., p. 30.

Since then, the program has remained largely on track. Development of the RBE2 radar has caused some technical-problem delays. In addition, budgetary shortfalls have led to schedule slippage in the planned delivery of the air force version, as well as in the development and testing of armaments such as the active radar MICA. Apart from these relatively minor delays and problems, however, the development program has proceeded smoothly. As of February 1994, Rafale prototypes had logged 1712 test flights. An additional 62 flights of the naval version were carried out in May 1994 during sea trials on the carrier *Foch*. Testing of the SNECMA M88 engine is proceeding according to schedule and specifications with 1560 flight test hours. Development and testing of the armament systems are continuing without major problems. In addition to the 2450 test flights carried out by Dassault, the test center of the French procurement agency has completed almost 5000 flights on four specially modified aircraft.[12]

In view of the large commitment of resources and extensive testing already expended, few French observers were surprised by the high priority the government assigned to Rafale in the new long-term defense plan. In April 1994, the French government approved the new *Loi de Programmation Militaire,* a six-year plan for military spending for the period 1995–2000.[13] The plan establishes a policy to "favor programs for which important financial commitments have already been made." The Rafale ACM (naval version) is explicitly placed in this category, as is the MICA missile. The *Loi de Programmation Militaire* also includes industrial policy, emphasizing the maintenance of manufacturing capabilities. Series production of both the Rafale ACM and ACT (air force version) are designated as key programs for achieving this end.

For budgetary reasons, the plan postpones the first operational squadron of 20 Rafales for the French air force until 2001, a delay of 18 months. The naval version, however, will be operational in 1999,

---

[12]See *Air & Cosmos*, February 14, 1994, No. 1459, pp. 22–25.

[13]See *Le Monde,* April 21, 22, 1994. The *Loi de Programmation Militaire* can be found in the annex to the *Journal Officiel,* June 24, 1994, p. 9095. For detailed accounts, see also Jac Lewis, "French plan bucks trend in defence budget cuts," *Jane's Defence Weekly,* International Edition, May 7, 1994, p. 15, as well as "French programming law to set growth at 0.5%," *International Defence Review,* June 1, 1994, p. 6.

as scheduled, together with the new aircraft carrier *Charles de Gaulle*. The law explicitly authorizes procurement funding for one squadron—20 aircraft—of Rafale ACT and one "*flotille*" (aircraft carrier flight) of 12 Rafale ACM for the French navy. Furthermore, procurement of 240 MICA missiles is authorized, along with a number of powered Apache stand-off weapons dispensers.

The six-year program law appears to reflect a wide political consensus in France and a strong commitment to the program by the French political establishment. Both military experts and the political leadership know the French armed services desperately need to update their aging fighter inventories, and nothing suggests that the government has seriously considered alternatives to Rafale since it forced the navy some years ago to stop examining the McDonnell-Douglas F/A-18 as a possible gap filler until the Rafale ACM came on line. [14]

Of course, the strong French commitment to complete development and launch series production of the Rafale should not be viewed only in terms of military requirements but also as direct support to the French aerospace and electronics industries. In February 1994, the French government issued its first Defense White Paper in 22 years.[15] Noting that military-related industries constitute 5 percent of industrial employment, 7 percent of total industrial output, and 5 percent of exports, the White Paper calls for a "new spirit of partnership between the State and the concerned enterprises."[16] After the publication of the *Loi de Programmation Militaire*, Defense Minister Léotard stated: "I have reduced spending on infrastructure for the armed forces to help the industrial sector. Industrial capabilities will be maintained, all procurement programs will be kept up . . . The first choice is to give manufacturing priority."[17]

---

[14]See Mark Lorell, *The Future of Allied Tactical Fighter Forces in NATO's Central Region*, RAND, R-4144-AF, 1992.

[15]The last White Paper was published in 1972, under President Pompidou. *Livre Blanc sur la Défense—1994, La Documentation Française.*

[16]Ibid., p. 160.

[17]Quoted in "French Military Budget Supports Defence Industry," *Reuter News Service—Western Europe*, April 28, 1994.

Every indication suggests the French government will stick to this "new spirit of partnership" and procure close to the originally planned total of 336 Rafales (250 Rafale ACTs for the air force and 86 Rafale ACMs for the navy),[18] at a planned procurement rate of 16 aircraft a year.[19] The huge resources already committed to the program, the great need of the air force and especially the navy for a new fighter, and the high priority placed on industrial policy by the government make cancellation of the program or a greatly truncated production run highly unlikely.

EF-2000: GUARDED OPTIMISM FOR A TROUBLED PROGRAM

Of the three European aircraft development projects under review, the EF-2000 project's long-term prospects are the most uncertain. Indeed, with schedule slippage now surpassing two and one-half years, escalating costs, large reductions in planned procurement numbers, and particularly strong opposition to the program in Germany, many observers remain doubtful that the program can survive into full production. We argue, however, that the EF-2000 will likely be fully developed, produced, and procured, although possibly not with the full participation of all the current participants. We perceive an unshakable commitment of Britain to the program, and full recognition of the very high political, economic, and technological costs of cancellation to Germany and the other partners.

The current Eurofighter program took shape after the departure of the French in July 1985, when the four remaining governments readjusted the share holdings to 33 percent each for Germany and Britain, 21 percent for Italy, and 13 percent for Spain. The participating industry and government teams completed the project definition phase in September 1986, after which the definitive ESR-D (European Staff Requirement-Development) was issued in Septem-

---

[18]Ibid.

[19]Defense Minister François Léotard, answering a question by defense specialist Olivier Darrason, MP, said that he was planning to allocate more funding to the industrialization of the Rafale after the year 2000 and increase yearly production to 20 aircraft a year. See Le Monde, July 1, 1994, p. 12.

ber 1987.[20] The full-scale development contract was authorized in 1988. Eurofighter was then the most visible program of European arms procurement cooperation.

Yet by 1991, the first Eurofighter prototype still had not flown. The two test aircraft had been grounded in Germany and Great Britain because of developmental problems with the flight control system. The changed security environment and growing budgetary constraints prompted German Defense Minister Volker Rühe to reassess the program. Plagued with embarrassing technical problems, the program came under withering criticism in the Federal Republic for its high costs and its alleged lack of relevance in the post–Cold War European environment. In the summer of 1992, Rühe threatened to pull Germany out of the project after the completion of R&D. At this time, it was widely reported that the Eurofighter was all but dead. In an attempt to save the program, the four-nation consortium undertook two major studies—one by the chiefs of staff to review the original operational requirement, and a second by industry to identify potential cost reductions.[21]

In October 1992, the consortium presented alternative design and cost reduction proposals to the German government. At a conference of defense ministers held the next month, Germany agreed to stay in the program if a major restructuring was accepted. The conference decided to rename the joint aircraft the Eurofighter EF-2000, to emphasize the restructuring and newly delayed production schedule. Under the new program, the launch of production was moved back to 1997, with first deliveries to Italy and the UK slated for 2000. Deliveries to Spain will start in 2001 and Germany in 2002. In addition, all the partners except Britain slashed their original planned procurement numbers: Germany down to 140 from 250, Italy at 130 instead of 165, and Spain with 87 compared to 100. Britain remained committed to its original planned buy of 250. These cuts slashed the original total buy of 765 to 607.[22] Participants

---

[20]See *Jane's All the World's Aircraft*, 1993.

[21]Defence Committee, Third Report, *Progress on the Eurofighter 2000 Programme, 1994*, HMSO, p. v.

[22]See "Four Nations Face Choices," *Aviation Week & Space Technology*, May 23, 1994, p. 44.

delayed the determination of final production numbers until 1995 after the fall elections in Germany. Equally important, Germany and Spain opted—at least initially—to procure lower-capability versions of the aircraft to save costs. These two countries decided to procure off-the-shelf avionics and to withdraw from the expensive DASS program, in the hopes of reducing the unit price tag by 30 percent.[23] Britain and Italy confirmed their commitment to the original performance specifications and equipment.[24]

In response to calls for restructuring the program, the British Parliament launched an exhaustive review of the Eurofighter effort.[25] The House of Commons established a multiparty commission to hold hearings and receive testimony from government and industry program officials. BAe and DRA conducted extensive combat simulations and other studies to evaluate various options, and reported the results to the commission. In 1994 the commission reached its conclusions: Procurement of the EF-2000, in the quantities originally planned and with its full capabilities and equipment left intact, was necessary for the RAF to carry out its assigned security tasks and meet the new post–Cold War threats associated with possible instability in Eastern Europe and uncertainty in the Middle East.

Despite delays, seemingly endless political wrangling, and cost overruns, the program received a major boost in March 1994 when the first EF-2000 finally flew in Germany, followed a week later by the first flight of the British prototype. As of May 1994, both prototypes

---

[23]*Jane's All the World's Aircraft*, 1993. Both British simulations and a study conducted by the German Federal Comptrollers Board, the BRH, indicate that EF-2000's combat performance will be significantly reduced by eliminating the DASS and other equipment. However, the official German position is that Germany will either develop its own national EW system or rejoin Eurodass (a consortium of European companies developing the DASS) at some later date. See Heinz Schulte, "Eurofighter funds will fall short, says report," *Jane's Defence Weekly*, International Edition, August 6, 1994, p. 3.

[24]However, Italy did decide not to equip its version of the EF-2000 with a laser warning device as part of the DASS.

[25]Defence Committee, Third Report, *Progress on the Eurofighter 2000 Programme, 1994*, HMSO, p. v.

had accumulated 10 hours each.[26] The initial flight-test program ended at that point, in preparation for the launch of a much more extensive second phase of flight testing.

Will the recent restructuring of the program and the beginning of flight testing save the Eurofighter? We believe EF-2000 will survive in some form, for a variety of reasons. Among the most important are the pressing need of the participating air forces for new fighters and the negative political and economic consequences of cancellation for the European military aerospace industry.

The RAF needs to replace its already retired F-4 Phantoms, its Jaguars, and eventually its Tornados. Germany must replace its aging F-4s; Italy its F-104S Starfighters, and Spain its F-4s and Mirage F-1s and 3s.[27] Without EF-2000, these air forces will eventually be forced to buy something else. The only feasible options will be American aircraft, Russian fighters, or the Rafale. None of these options appear to be fully palatable to the participating countries either politically or economically.

Of the $13 billion the four governments allocated for the development phase, three-fifths has already been expended.[28] Little of this money could be recovered or applied to an alternative aircraft procurement solution if EF-2000 is canceled. Licensed production of a foreign aircraft would require major new industrial start-up investments. An off-the-shelf purchase would eliminate thousands of skilled jobs and devastate the high-technology aerospace sectors of four countries.

Perhaps more important than the money already spent or the need for new fighters (which could be bought elsewhere), the EF-2000 is likely to be developed and procured because of the jobs it provides and the support it offers to the industrial base.

---

[26]See Carole A. Shifrin, "Eurofighter Partners Debate Program Issues," *Aviation Week & Space Technology*, May 23, 1994, p. 42.

[27]Ibid.

[28]Rolf Soderland, "Germany Asks Eurofighter Developers for Final Price," *Reuter News Service—Western Europe*, November 9, 1993.

Germany's Deutsche Aerospace has been particularly hard hit by the decline in defense expenditures and the problems with Eurofighter. Between 1990 and 1995, it will have cut its workforce from 14,000 to 5000.[29] Deutsche Aerospace is heavily dependent on EF-2000 and Airbus for continued survival. It is thus no surprise that, in order to save jobs at the company's facilities in Munich, the first EF-2000 prototype was not sent to Warton, England, to continue flight testing as originally planned. Despite Minister Rühe's rhetoric, the German government is well aware of the importance of the aerospace industry in the German economy.[30]

Although Chancellor Kohl's ruling coalition was weakened by the outcome of the October 1994 elections, it was unlikely that the new government would become more hostile to EF-2000. Even had the Social Democrat Party (SPD) won a clear victory in October's elections, it is far from certain that a more left-wing government in Bonn would undercut the remaining jobs at Deutsche Aerospace and eliminate Germany's military aerospace industry capabilities by canceling EF-2000. Indeed, in the early 1970s the SPD was inalterably opposed to the continuation of Eurofighter's predecessor, the collaborative Tornado attack fighter. But when the party finally came into power, it quickly reassessed its position because of the jobs question, and the Tornado continued on into full production.

Yet a German commitment to continue with Eurofighter production remains far from certain. Volker Rühe's decision to speak out in public against the Eurofighter back in 1992 dramatically politicized the debate in Germany. It is unclear what policy the weakened Kohl government will eventually adopt.

Irrespective of the German decision, the British government, political establishment, and armed forces appear fully committed to going ahead with the program, alone if necessary. In its conclusion, the Third Report of the Defence Committee notes the vital importance of the EF-2000: "What our partner nations decide to do in order to se-

---

[29]Heinz Schulte, "Military Wings Over Germany," *Jane's Defence Weekly*, International Edition, May 28, 1994, p. 19.

[30]See the eight-point plan by the German government to rescue its aerospace industry. For details, see "Aiming High, Scoring Low," *Flight International*, November 10, 1993, p. 3.

cure savings is of course a matter for them: but it would be wholly unacceptable if the United Kingdom were to procure an aircraft known to be unable to match the threat."[31]

Furthermore, the RAF is seriously examining the possibility of procuring even more EF-2000s to replace virtually all its major combat fighter aircraft. This would raise the British procurement buy from 250 to 350, an increase of 40 percent.[32] Such a large extension of the production run could lower unit costs, stabilize employment, and maintain capabilities in the military aerospace sector for decades, while transforming EF-2000 into a viable effort even if Germany calls it quits. Under the current plan, EF-2000 will provide jobs for some 40,000 skilled workers in the United Kingdom alone. At the currently planned production rate of 12 to 15 aircraft per year, the Eurofighter will support these jobs for nearly two decades.[33]

Italy's continuing support of the program is based on its pressing need to replace its vintage F-104S Starfighters—a fighter originally developed in the early 1950s—and the great economic and technological importance of Eurofighter for the nation's industrial base. The Italian government has already spent more than 1500 billion lira ($945 million) on EF-2000 R&D. The R&D phase alone employs 4000 people in Italy; the production phase is projected to add 11,000 more skilled jobs,[34] for a total of 15,000 people and a projected total of 180 million work hours. In the economically depressed northern areas, the industrial heartland of Italy, such jobs are crucial. The EF-2000 program involves a total of 120 Italian firms, including 20 prime contractors. Indeed, the future viability of the Italian military aerospace sector is heavily dependent on the continuation of Eurofighter.

---

[31]Third Report, p. viii.

[32]The Ministry of Defence has commissioned the EF-2000 consortium to study the possibility of design changes to transform the Eurofighter into a tactical reconnaissance aircraft. The cost of this development project is to be born by the UK. See Third Report, p. ix.

[33]Giorgio S. Frankel, "Il Debuto di Eurofighter 2000—Il caccia alleato bombarda la crisi," *Mondo Economico*, May 14, 1994, p. 90.

[34]Assuming production of 130 EF-2000, including 19 two-seaters. See ibid.

Spain's plans for building up its national aerospace capabilities and acquiring advanced technologies useful throughout the economy are based on the EF-2000 effort. Spanish industry is acquiring far more technology and expertise than it could possibly gain through a licensed-production program for an American or other foreign fighter. For example, Spanish industry has been catapulted to the cutting edge of advanced composite materials technology through its extensive participation in the development and manufacture of Eurofighter's cocured carbon-fiber wing boxes. Therefore, Spain's continuing involvement is likely, as suggested by the recent optimism of Spanish Secretary of State for Defense, Antonio Flos Bassols, when he noted that the EF-2000 has reached "cruising speed, having surmounted the difficulties that resulted in the four countries deferring schedules and downgrading their specifications."[35]

It therefore seems likely that the program will survive in some form, probably with the Germans, but even without them. As German Defense Minister Volker Rühe likes to point out, the EF-2000 is still under development and no decision regarding procurement has yet been made, although canceling the program when development work is practically finished could prove politically difficult. What could have been done in 1992 could be much harder to achieve three years later—after an additional DM 740 million ($466.2 million) has already been spent.[36] With tens of thousands of jobs and the future viability of much of Europe's military aerospace sector at stake, it is difficult to imagine that Eurofighter will not be procured.

---

[35]See, Rene Luria, "Spain walks the budget tightrope," *International Defense Review*, July 1, 1994, p. 2.

[36]Rolf Soderlind, "Germany Asks Eurofighter Developers for Final Price," *Reuter News Service—Western Europe*, November 9, 1993.

Chapter Five

WILL THE FIGHTERS BE SOLD?

The "gray threat" can be taken seriously only if the new European fighters are likely to be sold in significant numbers outside of Europe. In the uncertain strategic global environment that is evolving in the wake of the Cold War, it is difficult to predict the likely sales prospects for these fighters. However, three basic points can be made. First, several of the key European governments and contractors involved in these programs appear to be more committed than ever before to promoting foreign sales and seem determined to do whatever it takes to win export orders. Second, the export price of these fighters will likely be broadly competitive with U.S. fighters available for export. Third, a large potential market outside of Europe exists. As a result, it is probable that major export orders for one or more of the new European fighters will eventually be won.

SWEDISH GOVERNMENT AND INDUSTRY FIGHTER EXPORT POLICIES

Harsh economic and political realities appear to be bringing about a sea change in the Swedish government's policy toward arms exports, at least in the case of Gripen. In the post–Cold War environment, the Swedish government hopes to maintain a strong and independent military aerospace industrial base, while seeking closer economic and political collaboration with the rest of Europe. In support of this strategy, Sweden is moving toward a far more aggressive export posture on Gripen than was typical on past national programs, while actively seeking marketing arrangements with other European countries having strong export records. For the first time, the Swedish government and industry are examining a dedicated variant called the JAS-39X explicitly optimized for the export market.[1] This variant could be considerably more capable than the initial Gripen versions entering service in the Swedish Air Force.

A possible purpose of this variant would be to reduce U.S. influence over the countries to which Sweden exports its new fighter. Swedish Defense Minister Andreas Bjorck is a strong advocate of exporting Gripen. He has recently engaged in a protracted argument with U.S. authorities regarding export of the new fighter. Because the U.S. content of Gripen stands at between 26 percent and 40 percent, depending on which weapons, training simulators, and the like that a particular customer chooses, American authorities can block exports of the fighter. Some Swedish officials are concerned that the U.S. government would delay or halt Gripen exports in order to favor a competing American fighter. Sweden insisted on receiving a "green light giving solid guarantees that exports to certain countries would be approved."[2] Without such assurances, Sweden threatened to increasingly reduce the U.S. content in the fighter and purchase non-U.S. munitions. This issue appears to have been satisfactorily resolved, permitting the long-delayed sale of AIM-120 AMRAAM missiles to finally take place. The sale agreement reportedly includes "a provision that export versions of the JAS-39 Gripen can carry the AIM-120."[3]

Swedish industry is also actively and openly seeking to expand its military exports. The Swedish consortium producing Gripen—IG JAS—is turning to export markets to increase total production numbers and reduce unit costs. Saab-Scania restructured its operations by separating its civil airliner and defense businesses, and "pulled together its defence activities into one unit."[4] The Saab-Scania CEO,

---

[1]See "Sweden: Combat Aircraft Directory—SAAB Scania JAS 39 Gripen," *Flight International,* July 13, 1994, p. 51. See below for more information concerning export plans.

[2]See Simon Haydon, "Sweden Attacks US on Fighter Jet Export procedure," *Reuter News Service—Western Europe,* April 27, 1994.

[3]Theresa Hitchens, "Sweden Selects AMRAAM Over French Missile," *Defense News,* August 11, 1994.

[4]Charles Bickers, "Saab goes on the offensive," *Jane's Defence Weekly,* International Edition, April 30, 1994, p. 29.

Lars Kylberg, recently said that Gripen was "the company's major defence export product" and expressed his desire "to find an international collaborative partner to help market, produce and expand the aircraft system."[5] Saab has discussed this option with Northrop and Dassault, in addition to BAe.

The marketing negotiations between BAe and IG JAS are the most promising. The Saab Military Aircraft president sees a "50 per cent chance of having a marketing agreement."[6] Although the content of the negotiations has not been made public, industry analysts point to the "perfect match" between BAe and IG JAS. Indeed, the Swedes need the British marketing clout, while the British seek some welcome additional development and production work. BAe believes Gripen could fit well in its overall marketing portfolio. The export JAS-39X would be a convenient upper-range light-combat aircraft positioned between the top-end EF-2000 and the lower-range Hawk 100/200 series.[7] The two companies have discussed replacing the American F404 engine with a version of the EJ200 used on Eurofighter. This would enhance Gripen's performance, provide more development work for BAe and Saab, lower costs for EF-2000, and reduce U.S. influence over Swedish exports. In February 1994, the Swedish Defense Minister and his British counterpart, Malcolm Rifkind, signed a Memorandum of Understanding giving their governments' stamp of approval to the ongoing negotiations between Saab and BAe.

FRANCE AND THE EUROFIGHTER PARTNERS

With a market share of approximately 10 percent, France is the world's third largest exporter of arms. Over the past two decades, it has exported 35 percent of its production of conventional armaments. This represents some 5 percent of total French exports and more than 15 percent of the exports of durable goods.

The French government views arms exports as important both in terms of trade and as a critical means of financing and maintaining

---

[5]Ibid.

[6]Ibid.

[7]See *Flight International*, February 9, 1994, p. 13.

an independent defense industrial base. Arms exports have allowed France to "achieve its policy of independence in terms of arms procurement despite the limitations stemming from the very size of the country and its armed forces."[8] Furthermore, as noted in the 1994 French Defense White Paper, the government considers that "exports have been an instrument of foreign policy and French *présence* in the world."[9] In short, France's military export sales "have been instrumental in obtaining longer production runs, reducing program costs and easing national budgetary restraints."[10]

Historically, Dassault has exported a large percentage of its military aircraft production, with strong support from the French government. Entirely new versions of fighters have been developed for specific foreign customers, such as the Mirage 5 variant of the Mirage III for the Israeli Air Force. Favored foreign customers have received upgraded and more-capable versions of fighters before they were available to the French air force, as in the case of the Mirage 2000.

However, with the end of the Cold War, the French defense industry has suffered a serious decline in foreign sales, contributing to a loss of 100,000 jobs since 1990. Over the last decade, French aerospace companies have been losing long-time customers. The key Middle Eastern market has slipped from the French grip. In the 1980s, this region represented 70 percent of French aerospace exports, but by 1993 had fallen to only 10 percent.[11]

To help reverse these trends and permit France to pursue its policy of *independence nationale,* the French government has developed a new strategy to support the export activities of French defense companies. The action plan, as laid out in the Defense White Paper, contains four major elements: (1) increase the involvement of the military in export sales, (2) improve the system of guaranteed credits for foreign customers, (3) improve the coordination between civilian and defense industries to offer better industrial offset packages, and

---

[8]See *Livre blanc sur la Défense,* Documentation Française, 1994, p. 164.

[9]Ibid.

[10]"Arms Industry to Lose 100,000 Jobs Between 1990 and 1995," *Les Echos,* May 5, 1993, p. 12.

[11]"Dubai: French Aeronautics Companies Out in Force at Dubai Air Show," *Le Figaro,* November 11, 1993, p. 42.

(4) provide French defense companies greater direct governmental and political support.[12]

Enhancing exports of Rafale will almost certainly be a major target for this new action plan. Both the government and industry know that the long-term economic viability of both the Rafale program in particular and the French military aerospace industry in general require major foreign sales. The government is likely to push those sales aggressively worldwide, offering particularly attractive incentives to potential customers with respect to technology transfer, credits, and industrial offsets.

In the past, the French government has on occasion decided that the economic benefits of a foreign sale outweigh possible negative political considerations. Indeed, in the early 1980s the French continued to deliver Mirage F.1 fighters to Libya while preparing to engage in combat against rebel forces in Chad directly supported by the Libyan air force and army.[13] And, as is well known, France sold the Mirage F.1s and Exocet missiles to Iraq that were used during Desert Storm and that heavily damaged a U.S. Navy vessel prior to the war. In another conflict, the British had to cope with French, Israeli, and American fighters, as well as British combat ships, during the Falklands War. As one senior Dassault official told us,

> We will have to end up fighting our own armaments . . . Everyone
> has to worry about fighting everybody else's airplanes.

Many of the same considerations that are pushing the French to support export of Rafale apply equally to the Eurofighter partners. The problems encountered on the EF-2000 program with cost growth and declining procurement numbers increase the attractiveness and importance of foreign sales. Of the four major partners, the British government and BAe are likely to be the most aggressive promoters of foreign sales. Ministry of Defence and industry officials have made it clear that the British government plans to actively support export sales of the fighter. As already mentioned, BAe is also trying to

---

[12]*Livre blanc sur la défense,* op. cit., p. 165.

[13]See Mark Lorell, *Airpower in Peripheral Conflict: The French Experience in Africa,* RAND, R-3660-AF, 1989.

position itself with a diversified range of fighters through its negotiations with Saab, to broaden its offerings to foreign customers. The recent large-scale sale of the Tornado and Hawk aircraft to Saudi Arabia should serve as a reminder of the clout BAe and the British government can exercise.

Because of political constraints, Germany is likely to keep a low profile on foreign exports. Italy, however, has a strong record in military exports, and Spain will have little reason to oppose the others. All three of these partners, including Germany, will benefit from exports, no matter whose version is sold, and are therefore likely to be highly supportive of the UK's marketing efforts.

Finally, the Europeans have an export advantage in technology transfer. Historically, European defense contractors competing against American firms have often been able to compensate for lower-capability systems by offering the customer less-restricted access to technology. With the new generation of European fighters, the gap between American and European systems is closing. And although the U.S. government has recently eased its restrictions on technology transfer, it is likely that European firms will still be able to offer better deals in this area. In addition to assisting European sales, such a policy could contribute to an even greater proliferation of high-technology weapon systems and munitions.

COST

For the new European fighters to be attractive to potential foreign customers, they will need to be offered at a price that is reasonably competitive with alternative options available on the market. The Europeans can, of course, offset higher prices with better deals on technology transfer and industrial participation. Nonetheless, customers are unlikely to buy if the price demanded by the Europeans is dramatically higher than the price of other available fighters with roughly comparable capabilities. The most direct competitors to the European fighters will undoubtedly be versions of existing U.S. fighters, which have historically enjoyed a cost advantage resulting from much higher overall production runs.

It is impossible to know what price the Europeans will ask for a given fighter in a specific future market situation. However, we assume—

perhaps naively—that the asking price will bear some relationship to the fighter's actual cost. However, since none of the European fighters—except for the Gripen—is yet in full production, it is difficult to arrive at accurate cost figures. In addition, export versions can be substantially different from domestic ones and export deals typically involve complicated compensation packages. However, an examination of the available cost figures, and a comparison of those figures with costs for current U.S. fighters, can provide a useful although very rough idea of the likely cost competitiveness of the European fighters, to help assess the European aircraft export prospects.

Gripen Costs

There is little published information on the unit cost of the JAS-39 Gripen. In the spring of 1993, the Swedish Parliament agreed upon a revised cost framework calculated by the FMV that placed the total program cost through 2001, including development and production, at SKr 60.8 billion. Assuming full production of the projected first two batches of 140 Gripens, this would give a total program unit cost of SKr 434.3 million ($74.2 million). This rather high figure appears to include spares, munitions, training, documentation, etc. for a fully armed Gripen.

However, with the devaluation of the Swedish Krona, the dollar exchange rate is now 8.2. Because 26 percent of the outstanding payments are linked to the U.S. dollar, the total cost of the program has gone up in terms of the Krona but overall is cheaper when expressed in U.S. dollars. Indeed, the Swedish Parliament now puts the total cost 5 to 6 billion Krona higher. Assuming an increase of SKr 6 billion, total cost would be SKr 66.8 billion, for an average total program cost per unit of SKr 477.1 million. At a dollar exchange rate of SKr 8.2, the dollar cost comes down to $58.2 million.[14] Although still a high figure, it is important to note that this number reflects full amortization of all development costs over the first 140 Gripens only. Future orders by the Swedish air force or foreign customers would then have to cover production costs only. Saab officials claim that program unit costs are projected at about $40 million. This figure

---

[14]See *Veckans Affarer*, January 1, 1994, p. 4.

probably assumes a second large production order following the current production batch of 110 fighters, as originally planned.

Saab estimates that it will sell Gripen at a much lower export price of around SKr 200 billion ($24.4 million).[15] Although not clearly specified, this figure seems to be the projected flyaway cost for the JAS-39X. The same cost can be inferred from quotes circulated in the Swedish press concerning the total cost for Austria to replace its fleet of Drakens with Gripens. Saab-Scania reportedly estimates total cost for replacing 24 Drakens at SKr 5 billion. Since this figure is from April 1994, it can be assumed that the figure is based on a dollar exchange rate of 8.2 to the Swedish Krona. The unit cost would therefore be SKr 208.3 million ($25.4 million). These figures closely match the numbers provided by Saab officials, who claim that unit flyaway cost will be about $25 million.

Rafale Costs

Similar uncertainties are encountered when attempting to estimate the cost of Rafale. The French armament board has estimated the total cost of the Rafale program at FFr 178 billion ($33 billion at an exchange rate of 5.4 FFr to the dollar). This cost includes development costs and production of 320 fighters. Total program unit cost would stand at FFr 300 million, or $55.5 million at a dollar exchange rate of 5.4 francs.[16] This cost apparently does not include spares and munitions, although no precise accounting is offered. The latest estimate by the French Ministry of Defense estimates the cost of an unequipped Rafale at FFr 315 million, or $58.3 million.[17]

However, other published estimates have been higher. Arthur Paecht, a defense specialist, reportedly told the finance committee of the French Parliament that total cost for 234 Rafales for the air force and 86 for the navy is FFr 257 billion, or $47.6 billion. In another study, he broke down the cost of the naval version of the

---

[15]Saab notes that this would be a third of the price of a F-22. See Simon Haydon, op. cit.

[16]"France boosts its Rafale order to five," *Jane's Defence Weekly*, International Edition, March 5, 1994, p. 30.

[17]Quoted by *AGEFI*, March 4, 1995, p. 4.

Rafale, FFr 13 billion for R&D and FFr 32 billion for production of 86 units, for a unit cost for the naval version of FFr 390.2 million, or $72.26 million at an exchange rate of 5.4 French francs to the dollar.[18]

EF-2000 Costs

The multinational aspect of the EF-2000 makes cost evaluations all the more complicated. Because each version is different, costs differ also. Differing exchange rates further complicate matters. Each participating government pays only its own contractors for their assigned tasks, and does not possess full data on the costs and expenditures of other partners. For simplicity's sake, we provide cost estimates primarily of the British and German versions, plus a brief reference to the likely cost of the Italian version.

The recent British parliamentary review of Eurofighter provided estimates of the development and production costs expected for a British program of 250 aircraft. Development costs are put at £3460 million and production costs for 250 aircraft at £8600 million. The total program cost amounts to £12,060 million for an average program unit cost of £48.2 million. As of July 1, 1994, however, Ministry of Defence procurement chief Malcolm McIntosh told Parliament that EF-2000 development costs had gone up by £395 million, for a total development cost of £3856 million.[19] At a dollar exchange rate of 1.52, average production cost would be $52.8 million and the total system unit cost would stand at $75.7 million. These numbers are summarized in Table 3.

The German costs are difficult to evaluate because of changing exchange rates and unclear data. The latest figure offered by Jorg Schonbohm, the German Secretary for Defense, is a unit cost of DM

---

[18]Jac Lewis, "France to cut R&D to fund equipment buys," *Jane's Defence Weekly*, International Edition, May 28, 1994, p. 6.

[19]"Eurofighter gets 200 million German marks; cost growth conceded," *Aerospace Daily*, July 1, 1994, p. 5A.

Table 3

Official British EF-2000 Costs for 250 Aircraft
(millions of £/$)

	Total	Average Per Unit
Development (UK share)	£3,856[a]	£15.4 ($23.4)
Production (250 aircraft)	£8,600	£34.4 ($52.8)
Total	£12,456	£49.8 ($75.7)
Fly-away cost[a]	£10,460	£41.8 ($63.5)

[a]Includes everything but R&D costs—production, integrated logistics support, and simulators and training aids for the 250 EF-2000 that the RAF requires. From *Jane's Defence Weekly*, International Edition, May 14, 1994.

102 million ($64.2 million at an exchange rate of DM/$ of 0.63).[20] The German government seeks to bring that figure down to under DM 100 million. However, the recent report by the German Federal Comptrollers Board estimates the unit cost now stands at DM 103 million ($64.9 million) and not the DM 90 million that Rühe's office had originally quoted to the Board. It is not obvious what these numbers represent, but the British parliamentary report clearly implies that they are not average program unit costs. It appears that the British version, which is more capable than the stripped-down German variant, now costs less in dollar terms because of the depreciation of the UK currency.

In any case, the final cost of the German version is far from clear. The German authorities were to announce their decision regarding the pursuit of the program early in 1995 and must announce production quantities in the third quarter of 1995. Until then, exact figures are hard to come by as each side of the political game tries to keep its options open.[21]

---

[20]Charles Bickers, "Ministers tight-lipped as EF-2000 takes bow," *Jane's Defence Weekly*, International Edition, May 14, 1994, p. 5.

[21]As of June 1995, German participation still appeared shaky according to press accounts. Germany apparently still has not made a firm committment to go ahead with the program.

Published estimates of the cost of the Italian version are close to the British flyaway cost shown above. According to one source, a "combat-ready" EF-2000, including logistical support, will cost between 95 and 100 billion Italian lira, or $59.85 million apiece with a dollar exchange rate of 0.00063 to the lira. This apparently excludes R&D, but includes basic spares, munitions, and the like.

Cost Comparisons

Using the costs calculated as discussed above for the new European fighters, Table 4 offers comparisons with current U.S. fighters that would be the most likely competitors in international markets. The estimates for both European and American fighters are not claimed in any way to be definitive or exactly comparable. They are only meant to provide a rough sense of the relative magnitude of differences in costs for the two sets of aircraft. As can be seen from Table 4, the European fighters are generally shown in the same cost range as U.S. fighters in broadly comparable performance categories. For example, the flyaway cost for Gripen appears to be quite similar to that of the F1-16C/D Block 40, while the same category of cost for Rafale and EF-2000 is in a range similar to that of the F-15E and F-18E/F.

Whatever the true costs of the European fighters, one thing is virtually certain: the European governments and contractors will price their aircraft to make them cost competitive with other aircraft available on the market. As one French industry official told us when asked what the MICA missile would cost for foreign customers, "MICA will sell for the same price as AMRAAM," whatever price that might be.

IS THERE AN EXPORT MARKET OUTSIDE OF EUROPE?

Developing a detailed international market forecast for new fighters goes far beyond the scope of this study. We limit ourselves to three general points. First, the European contractors have commissioned studies that show a large potential market, although they may be overly optimistic. Second, a significant number of air forces around the world clearly will need to replace fighters over the next 10 to 15

Table 4

**Fighter Cost Comparisons
(millions of U.S. dollars)[a]**

European	Flyaway Cost	Program Cost[b]	Program Unit Cost	Total Unit Procurement Cost[c]
Gripen	$24.4[d]	$8,000[e]	$58.2	
Rafale[f]	$58.3[g]	$33,000[h]	$103[i]	
EF-2000[j]	$52.8[k]	$18,900	$75.7	$63.5[l]
U.S.[m]				
F-15E[n]	$49			$63
F-16C/D[o]	$24			$32
F-18E/F[p]	$54			$67
F-18C/D[q]	$30–34			$38–43

[a]It is important to note that prices for U.S. aircraft do not include R&D costs because they have been amortized for the most part. Export prices will undoubtedly be different, since each export deal varies and compensation or trade-off packages may not be represented in the export price.

[b]Program cost includes all R&D and production costs.

[c]Unit procurement cost is found by adding to the flyaway cost the costs of initial spares, peculiar support equipment, training materials, technical data, etc.

[d]SKr 200 million Saab estimate, April 1994.

[e]SKr 66.8 billion. Cost estimate from Swedish Parliament, January 1994.

[f]Average cost of air force and naval version.

[g]FFr 315 million. Estimate from French Ministry of Defense, April 1994.

[h]FFr 178 billion. Official cost quoted by French armament board, May 1994.

[i]FFr 556.3 million. The production run of only 320 aircraft renders the proportion of embedded R&D cost much higher than for the EF-2000, which has an almost 100 percent larger production run.

[j]Cost to UK only of UK version.

[k]This figure represents production costs only.

[l]This cost includes all costs other than R&D or for the preliminary industrialization phase—i.e., in addition to production, integrated logistics support, simulators, and training aids required by the RAF.

[m]Costs indicated are RAND calculations, based on published data from Defense Department System Acquisition Reports. Prices are FY94 to U.S. military buyers.

[n]F-15E with Lantirn and other government-furnished equipment (GFE), which would not be included in export versions. Assumes low production rates.

[o]Block 50. Assumes low production rates.

[p]Cumulative average for 540 units.

[q]Cost range for FY89–93 buys, quantities of 36 to 84 per year.

years. Finally, at least some of the European contractors are already discussing possible sales with foreign countries.

Eurofighter executives "put the worldwide export market for EFA (now EF-2000)-class aircraft at some 3,000 aircraft between 1991 and 2015."[22] Chairman Serge Dassault has forecast a market for "600 aircraft in the coming years."[23] Taking out the 324 units to be procured in France, this suggests an anticipated export market of about 300 aircraft in the "coming years."

How realistic are these projections? A recent study suggests that, at least in the case of the Rafale, they are overly optimistic.[24] The author conducted a detailed country-by-country analysis of potential customers, for the purpose of determining a total production run and thus likely unit cost. Cost estimates are based on three demand forecasts. The low estimate assumes no foreign sales at all. The middle (or "best-guess") estimate forecasts the export of 50 fighters, and the high estimate forecasts 190 aircraft.

It is arguable, however, that the sales projections in this study may be too conservative. The study dismisses possible clients such as Pakistan and Iran, as well as several countries with growing economies in Southeast Asia and Latin America. The sale of only 40 Rafales is seen as likely to Middle Eastern countries (20 each for Kuwait and the United Arab Emirates [UAE]) and the former Soviet satellite countries are ignored. Although it appears today that such countries do not have the economic means to purchase one of the new European fighters, this situation may change.

Furthermore, the study generally ignores potential collaborative development arrangements that could transfer the technologies and capabilities of the European aircraft to foreign countries. With mainland China experiencing unprecedented economic growth, it is not implausible to imagine sales or codevelopment deals with the Europeans. Indeed, the press has persistently reported rumors that Israeli Aircraft Industries has helped the People's Republic of China

---

[22]*Aerospace Daily*, February 10, 1994, p. 219.

[23]"Dassault profits level," *Jane's Defence Weekly*, International Edition, June 18, 1994, p. 11.

[24]Yolande Simon, op. cit.

develop a new fighter prototype based on the Lavi. Dassault is already engaged in assisting India develop its light combat aircraft, which is reportedly a scaled-down version of Rafale.

Whatever the likely sales prospects, there is no doubt that the European governments and contractors are already actively engaged in trying to sell their new fighters. In addition to Austria and several other European countries, sales targets for Saab and the Swedish government include potential customers outside of Europe such as Chile. The case of Chile may be indicative of the type of environment the United States may have to increasingly cope with. Chile needs to replace its 1950s-vintage Hawker-Hunter fighter/attack aircraft by the end of the decade.[25] The Chileans reportedly would prefer to procure the Lockheed F-16, but the sale is being blocked by the U.S. government.[26] At the Chilean air show, FIDAE '94, held in March 1994, Lockheed "could get a license to display the F-16, but couldn't get a license to market it there," according to an industry source.[27]

Saab, however did not face such constraints and in fact opened a sales office in the Chilean capital. The Swedish company presented its Gripen as a "high-tech, low-cost alternative to the F-16."[28] Swedish officials marketed their fighter by arguing that the SAF and the Chilean air forces had similar missions, as well as emphasizing Gripen's expected reliability and maintainability.[29]

Whatever the outcome of this particular deal, Saab—with the support of the Swedish government and possibly BAe—will be active around the world competing head-to-head with the F-16 class of fighters.

BAe has been selling its combat version of the Hawk in East and South Asia. It is undoubtedly following up with sales pitches for the EF-2000. Dassault has already launched major sales efforts for Rafale

---

[25]See John Tirpak, "South America, a rising market, poses test for US policy," *Aerospace Daily*, May 27, 1994, p. 327. See also David M. North, "Chilean Air Force Seeks New Multirole Aircraft," *Aviation Week & Space Technology*, April 25, 1994, p. 44.

[26]David M. North, op. cit.

[27]Quoted in John Tirpak, op. cit.

[28]Ibid.

[29]Ibid.

in the Middle East.   The French company was very active at the Dubai show in November 1993, suggesting its desire to regain lost ground among the Gulf States.   Dassault just opened a office in Abu Dhabi, posting General Pierre Pacalon, communications director of the French company.   His mission will be to restore links with Kuwait and promote Rafale to potential customers such as Saudi Arabia, among others.[30]   Recently the French announced a large order (FFr 1.5 billion) from Qatar for MICA and other missiles, as well as self-protection electronic countermeasures systems.[31]   Dassault also opened an office in Taipei in August 1993, after selling 60 Mirage jet fighters to Taiwan in a deal reportedly worth $2.6 billion.[32]   Finally, Dassault is one of the competitors in the UAE bid for 80 advanced multirole fighter aircraft.

In short, although it is impossible to predict how well the new European fighters will fare, it seems virtually certain that some major sales outside of Europe will eventually be made.

---

[30]"Abu Dhabi: Dassault Aviation Sends Emissary to Promote Mirage and Rafale," *Les Echos*, September 1, 1994.

[31]"Qatar Orders Matra MICA and Magic 2 Missiles," *Asian Defence Journal,* October 1994.

[32]"Taiwan Mulls Cooperation with Dassault," *Reuter Newswire—Far East,* Reuter Economic News, August 27, 1993.

Chapter Six

SUMMARY OBSERVATIONS

We believe the arguments presented in this report indicate that the claim made by some U.S. Air Force and Defense Department officials that the new European fighters represent a potential "gray threat" deserves serious consideration by defense analysts. Our survey of open literature sources and discussions with European government and industry officials suggest that:

- The new European fighters and future upgrades, armed with new-generation munitions currently under development, are likely to be highly competitive in overall capabilities with existing U.S. fighters and their future variants.

- We believe that all three new European fighters will be fully developed and procured in significant numbers.

- The new fighters are likely to be sold outside of Europe because (1) the participating governments and contractors appear to be strongly committed to promoting foreign sales; (2) the fighters are likely to be priced competitively with U.S. aircraft; (3) the Europeans can be expected to place fewer restrictions on technology transfer and provide other economic incentives; and (4) a worldwide demand for new fighters exists.

We believe the United States should carefully evaluate its defense requirements and equipment needs in view of a possible future environment in which the "gray threat" will be real. In such an environment, the U.S. Air Force will need to deploy the highest capability equipment available. The F-22 appears to guarantee clear superiority in combat capability over any of the new European fighters, even as demonstrated by their developers' own combat simulations. Any other fighter on the horizon for the U.S. Air Force may come up short.